THOUGHT LEADERSHIP on Tourism, Resilience, and Sustainability in the 21st Century

THOUGHT LEADERSHIP
on Tourism, Resilience, and Sustainability in the 21st Century

EDMUND BARTLETT

GTRCMC
Global Tourism Resilience & Crisis Management Centre

IAN RANDLE PUBLISHERS
Kingston • Miami

First published in Jamaica, 2023 by
Ian Randle Publishers
16 Herb McKenley Drive
Box 686
Kingston 6
www.ianrandlepublishers.com

ISBN: 978-976-8286-93-2 (pbk)
ISBN: 978-976-8286-94-9 (epub)

Cataloguing-In-Publication Data available at the National Library of Jamaica

Cover Design by Lloyd Waller and Rod Hanson
Book Design by Ian Randle Publishers

Printed and Bound in the United States of America

CONTENTS

Foreword

Dr Taleb Rifai
Former Secretary General of the United Nations World Tourism Organization

This book provides a comprehensive analysis of the international travel industry, giving readers a fresh perspective on how to adapt to a dynamic landscape. It is a compilation of Bartlett's insights, each one a thought-provoking investigation of some part of tourism, from ocean economies that can be sustained to the important role that digital landscapes play in advancing the industry as a whole.

The book is neatly divided into eight sections, each of which focuses on a certain facet of tourism. Many different topics are covered, such as 'Resilient Tourism for Sustainable Ocean Economies: Building Jamaica's Premier Tourism Destination,' 'Resilient Tourism for Sustainability,' 'Building Tourism Resilience,' 'Jamaica's Tourism Landscape: A Viable Case,' 'Advancing Tourism in the Digital Landscape,' 'International Trade and Tourism,' 'Promoting Sustainability in Tourism,' and 'Cruise Tourism and Beyond.'

In-depth discussions of many topics are provided in separate chapters, allowing readers to learn all they need to know about the tourist sector. Bartlett's book covers a wide range of subjects important to industry experts, politicians, and everyone concerned with the future of tourism, from the importance of the private sector in building tourist resilience to the impact of international commerce on the sector.

Beyond the bounds of a simple book, *Thought Leadership on Tourism, Resilience and Sustainability in the 21st Century* acts as a guide for the future of the tourist industry. Anyone interested in understanding the ever-evolving tourist business and the methods necessary to ensure its resilience and sustainability should read this book.

Introduction

Tourism has long been hailed as a powerful tool for economic development, cultural exchange, and environmental conservation. The allure of pristine beaches, diverse marine life, and vibrant cultures draws millions of travellers to coastal destinations each year. Yet, the very success of the tourism industry has led to challenges that must be addressed urgently in the face of increasing environmental threats and global uncertainties. Against this background, this book, a compilation of essays on various aspects of tourism, delves into the multifaceted aspects of fostering resilience within the tourism sector and explores current trends in tourism, resilience, and sustainability amid global change and innovation. The tourist ecology is especially explored against the backdrop of the recent COVID-19 pandemic, which undoubtedly served as a catalyst of change in our usual approach to varied aspects of life, including the tourism sector.

This book comprises eight chapters, each delving into key dimensions of the overarching theme of resilience and sustainability within the context of the tourism sector. The chapters are designed to provide a comprehensive understanding of sustainable ocean economies, resilient tourism for sustainability, exploring the idea of building tourism resilience, examining Jamaica's tourism landscape, exploring how to advance tourism in the digital landscape, as well as to look at international trade and tourism, promoting sustainability in tourism, and cruise tourism and its prospects.

Chapter 1, **Sustainable Ocean Economies**, sets the stage by discussing the critical importance of sustainable ocean economies in the modern world. It highlights the interconnectedness of various sectors, including tourism, fisheries, shipping, and renewable energy, and explores how these sectors can collaborate to create a holistic approach to ocean-based economic growth. It makes mention of the various challenges to the tourism sector, such as climate change which induces sea-level rise, food insecurity, water shortages, extreme heat, saline intrusion into aquifers and general coastal degradation, severe hurricanes, beach erosion, flooding, biodiversity loss, critical infrastructure collapse, safety concerns and increasing insurance costs. This further underscores that the effective adoption of sustainable tourism hinges on environmental sustainability being a central consideration in the tourism product. Therefore, aspects such as building design, construction, transportation, marketing, entertainment, adventure, energy use, customer service, waste disposal, maintenance and the use of utilities must be considered. The chapter also delves into the resilience in the blue economy, which speaks to the sustainable use of ocean resources for economic growth, improved livelihoods and jobs, and ocean ecosystem health. It highlights how the ocean and marine systems are increasingly threatened by activities, including but not limited to shipping and transport, dredging, offshore drilling, deep-sea mining and over-fishing, while emphasizing the need for urgent and decisive resilience strategies.

Chapter 2, **Resilient Tourism for Sustainable Development**, defines and explores the concept of resilient tourism, examining how it differs from traditional tourism models. It considers resilience in the context of the recent COVID-19 pandemic, effectively highlighting the economic fallouts associated with the tourism sector being one of the hardest hit in the global economy. Using Jamaica as the primary reference point, it highlights how ministries, departments, and agencies were forced to pivot and establish innovative means of keeping the tourism sector afloat. It further delves into geopolitics, its role in managing the pandemic, and its impacts on tourism. The pandemic reinforced the idea of the state being the traditionally primary protector of society. Further, as one could expect, it also created uncertainties among global powers that wrestled with competing interests as they sought to protect both national interests against global developments. The exploration of resilient tourism for development also delved into tourism in the Caribbean region, effectively illuminating the economic signifance of the tourism sector to Caribbean countries, but of course, not failing to highlight the challenges that hinder greater prospects. The chapter further looks into a new tourism model that countries, including those in the Caribbean, can adopt. This model is one that establishes a tourism sector that has health and safety as its cornerstones, and seeks to harness the power of digitalization in providing improved tourism products, both in quality and quantity.

Chapter 3, **Building Tourism Resilience**, delves deeper into the strategies and practices that can enhance the resilience of tourism destinations. It reiterates the context of the pandemic and its impact on the tourism sector while drawing on aspects including but not limited to Jamaica's resilient corridors, an initative which is a key demonstration of a disciplined, focused, protocol-based, and data-driven blueprint for safe reopening of the tourism sector. In identifying strategies for building resilience, in this chapter, I switch focus from Jamaica and the wider Caribbean, to African Destinations, where tourism has been one of the key drivers of growth of the African continent, quite like other developing regions in the world. In fact, it highlights how tourism to African GDP was measured at USD 168 billion in 2019, equivalent to 7.1 per cent of total GDP. Tourism also generated close to twenty-five million jobs, while visitor expenditures generated USD61.3BN or 10.4 per cent of total exports. Unfortunately, however, despite being endowed with natural assets such as wildlife, marine life, and extensive natural attractions, the continent continues to receive only a small proportion of the people who travel globally. As such, the chapter presents several strategies that can be adopted to improve the performance of the tourism industry in Africa. In further exploring opportunities for building tourism resilience, I touch on the importance of micro-, small- and medium-sized tourism enterprises (SMTEs) to the sustenance and vitality of the tourism sector. Artisans and craft vendors, attractions and tours, transportation, beauty shops and textiles, duty-free stores, restaurants and eateries, bed and breakfasts, guest houses, farmers and distributors of hotel supplies are the backbone of the tourism sector, though often overlooked. To this end, I provide strategies and initiatives being used, and can be used to improve their capacities, and overall visibility in the tourism sector. I also delve into the role of the private sector in the tourism industry, effectively highlighting how, they too, through their specializations in marketing, booking, aviation, ground transportation, accommodations, gastronomy, entertainment and recreation, manufacturing, banking and financing, and e-commerce, form the backbone of the tourism sector, as any disruptions in the former impacts the latter, and vice versa.

Chapter 4, **Jamaica's Tourism Landscape: A Visible Case**, focuses specifically on Jamaica's tourism industry, tracing its evolution from a modest beginning to a global destination. It evaluates the successes and challenges faced by the Jamaican government and industry stakeholders in maintaining sustainable growth while preserving the natural and cultural assets that make the island unique. Tourism generates direct employment for approximately one hundred and seventy-five thousand Jamaicans and indirect employment for over three hundred and fifty-four thousand Jamaicans. At the same time, it is the single largest contributor to GDP, the main source of foreign revenues and one of the country's main sources of exports. Tourism drives 15 per cent of construction, 10 per cent of banking and finance, 20 per cent of manufacturing, and 21 per cent of utilities, as well as agriculture and fisheries. With its several decades of focus on tourism, the country boasts some of the world's finest offerings in luxury tourism and has been acknowledged accordingly, having been listed among the best destinations in the world and titled "Best Destination" in 2019.

Chapter 5, **Advancing Tourism in the Digital Landscape**, acknowledges that the digital era, undoubtedly catalysed by the pandemic, has transformed the way travellers research, plan, and experience their journeys. It examines the role of technology in enhancing the sustainability and resilience of tourism. It discusses how digital platforms have been used and can be used to promote responsible travel, improve destination management, and contribute to community empowerment. It touches on how digital technologies such as robotics, artificial intelligence, and human-robot interactions became significant components in managing of the spread of COVID-19 in medical facilities, airports, transportation and even hotels, restaurants, and recreational areas. In this regard, it acknowledges an understanding that failure to adopt these technologies leaves businesses, those in the tourism sector included, prone to shocks that could otherwise be mitigated or reduced. It adds that ICTs have become critical aspects of the tourism industry, effectively improving guest services, reservations, food and beverage management, sales, food service catering, maintenance, security, and hospitality accounting. In the same breath, the chapter gives special focus to multi-destination in tourism. It is mentioned that international tourism trends now illustrate a shift from the traditional 'sun, sea and sand' towards interactive experiential tourism, as international tourists are now desiring to maximize their travel experiences by exploring as many sites, attractions, and locales as possible. This, then, accounts for the significance of the development of multi-destination arrangements. A multi-destination arrangement is based on joint partnerships involving governments, airlines, hotels, tour operators and attractions that will enable visitors to seamlessly travel two, three or more geographically proximate nations and stay over in each destination. Adopted in the Caribbean, multi-destination arrangements are one way of deepening regional integration.

Chapter 6, **International Trade and Tourism**, explores the intricate relationship between international trade and tourism, emphasizing how sustainable tourism practices can be integrated into trade policies to promote both economic growth and environmental protection. It discusses the potential benefits of aligning trade and tourism agendas to foster resilient economies. It gives special focus to regional integration in the Caribbean, identifying prospects for encouraging harmonization and coordination in the tourism sector, and towards efforts to encourage resilience and sustainability in the Caribbean, the most tourism-dependent region in the world. The chapter also establishes the significance of political leadership to resilience and sustainability in the tourism sector. Highlighting political leadership with the context of the recent pandemic, attention is given to the political leadership in Jamaica, which consisted of swift action, proactive leadership, effective communication, and innovative thinking, which led to the quick implementation of health and safety protocols which were crucial in guiding the tourism sector's management of the pandemic in accordance with globally accepted standards. This section of the chapter, generally, emphasizes that the success of the tourism sector heavily relies on effective political leadership which dictates the establishment of the necessary policies for the sector to stay afloat. In the same context of international trade and tourism, the chapter features a discussion of the global inclusive growth and tourism, which importantly highlights the interconnection of various sectors within the economy that affects the success of the tourism sector. In this regard, it mentions vital economic linkages, including manufacturing, agriculture, services, and the cultural and creative industries.

Chapter 7, **Promoting Sustainability in Tourism**, investigates the role of policies and partnerships in promoting sustainability within the tourism sector. It showcases examples of successful collaborations among governments, non-governmental organizations, and businesses, illustrating how these partnerships can drive positive change in the industry. The chapter emphasizes that there needs to be firm commitment among policymakers, industry leaders, and other tourism stakeholders to support a change in policies, business practices, and consumer behaviour towards a more sustainable tourism sector. This can contribute to the attainment of the Universal 2030 Agenda for Sustainable Development and the Sustainable Development Goals (SDGs), particularly in critical areas including but not limited to promoting inclusive and sustainable economic growth, social inclusiveness, employment and poverty, as laissez-faire models of tourism have proven dated in the context of recent changes and innovations. It notes that stakeholders must become more proactive, vigilant, and must constantly evaluate their capacities to counter old and emergent challenges. In the same breath, the chapter explores the significance of insurance, which is arguably an often overlooked area in the discussion of tourism sustainability. It emphasizes the need for two main types of insurance: parametric insurance and travel insurance, hastening to note that Jamaica has charted its way in providing travel insurance, thus becoming even more an attractive destination for tourists who seek the sort of security it provides. At the same time, the chapter introduces the reader to the concepts of anthropause to antropulse, noting that while COVID-19 restrictions led to a period of anthropause, the post-COVID period or the anthropulse period has threatened previous environmental gains as people try to make up for lost time during the pandemic, thereby accelerating environmental degradation. In this regard, there is increased emphasis on decisive strategies and actions to ensure that the tourism sector adopts sustainable practices.

Chapter 8, **Cruise Tourism and Beyond**, the final chapter of the book, examines the complex landscape of cruise tourism, a segment that presents unique challenges and opportunities for resilience and sustainability. It discusses innovative approaches to addressing the environmental and social impacts of cruise tourism while harnessing its potential for economic growth. The chapter also further explores multidestination, giving special attention to the opportunities and challenges. It notes the significance of gaining competitive advantage and enhancing sustainability through Caribbean countries' packaging and marketing their varied attractions more cohesively to entice potential visitors, further presenting an opportunity for regional destinations to tap into new markets by promoting the natural, historic, and cultural attributes of each country.

In total, this book provides readers with a comprehensive perspective on the multifaceted nature of a resilient and sustainable tourism sector, as it aims to inspire and inform stakeholders, policymakers, researchers, and enthusiasts alike to shape the future of tourism in ways that are not only economically beneficial but also environmentally and socially responsible. Through collaborative efforts and innovative strategies, we can pave the way for a more resilient, vibrant, and sustainable global tourism industry.

1.
Sustainable Ocean Economies

1.1. Sustainable Ocean Economies

Projections of accelerated climate change impacts on the global economy in the coming years indicate an urgent need for international tourism to transition towards a more balanced and sustainable sector. Such sector needs to address the central challenges of how scarce natural resources can be prudently managed and how economic growth can be aligned with the preservation of both land- and marine-based natural resources. This model emphasizes values such as sustainable consumption and production or the use of services and related products in a way that responds to basic needs and ensure a better quality of life while minimizing the use of natural resources and toxic materials, as well as the emission of waste and pollutants. The entire notion of sustainable tourism also calls for environmental sustainability to be built into all aspects of the tourism product – building design, construction, transportation, marketing, entertainment, adventure, energy use, customer service, waste disposal, maintenance, and the use of utilities.

As the tourism minister of Jamaica, a small-island state geographically situated among a cluster of other small islands, I am well-positioned to acknowledge the unquantifiable benefits of healthy marine and coastal ecosystems to the economic vitality of entire populations. A 2016 study by the World Bank estimated the economic value of the Caribbean Sea's coastal and marine ecosystems at US$54.55 billion. Indeed, the Caribbean Sea, which encircles the Caribbean region and is the second largest region of the Atlantic Ocean, is a valuable source of food, income, trade and shipping, minerals, energy, water supply, recreation, and tourism for Caribbean economies. The coral reef-mangrove-seagrass complex also brings increased safety to coastal communities as the systems act as a natural barrier, decreasing the impact of floods and storms. The Caribbean Sea is considered the 'high-diversity heart' of the Tropical West Atlantic; and without coral reefs, it has been estimated that 25 per cent of all marine life would die.

To prepare for their future and to enhance their competitiveness, global tourist destinations must urgently prioritize climate change action and mitigation. From the perspective of my own country, the tourism industry is very climate sensitive, and like most Caribbean islands, Jamaica's main tourism product is coastal, centred on 'sun, sea and sand.' The island and the tourism sector is, therefore, susceptible, whether directly or indirectly, to many risks posed by climate change, including sea-level rise, food insecurity, water shortages, extreme heat, saline intrusion into aquifers and general coastal degradation, severe hurricanes, beach erosion, flooding, biodiversity loss, critical infrastructure collapse, safety concerns, and increasing insurance costs. In general, climate change and global warming are the most urgent threats to global tourism, impacting all dimensions of an attractive tourism product – sand, sea, sun, food and people.

To promote a sustainable ocean economy and pushback against the various threats to healthy coastal and marine ecosystems, Ocean Action is urgently required as ocean health continues to rapidly decline. As its main strategy for building sustainable ocean economies, which are economic models that promote effective protection, sustainable resource use and production and equitable prosperity simultaneously, the Ocean Panel, comprising of 16 world leaders, has already set the ambitious target of achieving 100 per cent sustainable management of the ocean areas under national jurisdictions.

To demonstrate their commitment to this goal, all members of the Ocean Panel have released a joint statement to the United Nations Ocean Conference, urging all countries to harness the power of the ocean as a catalyst to deliver on all seventeen sustainable development goals and to mobilize financing for developing states to enhance their capacity to transition to sustainable ocean economies. This missive recognizes that global cooperation and coordination among a wide-ranging number of stakeholders will be one of the most crucial success factors in reconstructing the actions and ethos of industries, including tourism, to achieve improved management of the activities that most significantly harm the ocean, its resources, and ecosystems.

The transition to sustainable ocean economies will also require a set of concrete ideas, strategies, best practices, and policies that can be standardized and operationalized by all stakeholders. In this regard, I acknowledge the tremendous instructional value of the new Ocean Panel–commissioned report entitled *Opportunities for Transforming Coastal and Marine Tourism: Towards Sustainability, Regeneration and Resilience*. The report provides the framework for the realization of the sustainable goal set by the Ocean Panel that by 2030: 'Coastal and ocean-based tourism is sustainable, resilient, addresses climate change, reduces pollution, supports ecosystem regeneration and biodiversity conservation and invests in local jobs and communities.'

Harnessing the perspectives of over forty experts, this toolkit constitutes an unprecedented body of information on sustainable coastal and marine tourism, generating a comprehensive understanding of marine and coastal tourism across the world and showcasing the global scale and impact of the opportunities and benefits that can be realized by transforming the coastal and marine tourism industry.

My contribution to the report focused on cruise tourism as a segment of the coastal and marine tourism industry. I underscored that coastal and marine tourism is a major driver of economic growth and job creation in the Caribbean, especially through cruise tourism as the Caribbean is among the world's leading ocean cruise destinations, holding over 40 per cent of the global market share since 2017. In Jamaica, for example, the Jamaican economy earned an average of US$174.5 million through cruise tourism, pre COVID-19. At the same time, I also acknowledged that the cruise tourism industry produces a significant environmental impact.

Environmentally, the impacts associated with large cruises include the emission of greenhouse gases, which contribute to climate change and waste from ships, which causes pollution and reduces the resilience of marine ecosystems and damage to fragile coastal and marine environment including corals. A 2021 report published in the Marine Pollution Bulletin found that a large cruise liner can produce a bigger carbon footprint than twelve thousand cars, while an overnight stay onboard uses twelve times more energy than a stay in a hotel. Against this backdrop, it has become important to balance the economic gains to be derived from the blue economy with the biodiversity conservation and the sustainable use of marine and coastal resources, as well as the social impact on coastal communities.

To reduce its environmental impact, the cruise industry needs to continue to accelerate gains in four key areas: controlling emissions, sewage treatment, fuel efficiency, and recycling. While admittedly, the cruise tourism has recently demonstrated a much stronger commitment to maritime environmental protection and responsible tourism, with policies often exceeding those required by law, it is important that the cruise industry continues to undertake greater investment in research and development to develop the technologies and energy sources that will enable the cruise industry to pursue sustainable solutions, and that it continues to place a high priority on environmental compliance and systems for enforcement. Afterall, the health and sustainability of our oceans is critical to the survival of the tourism industry and, by extension, our planet. By this token, as a small island developing state, Jamaica fully endorses the goal of the Ocean Panel to achieve a sustainable tourism economy by 2030.

1.2. Resilience for Blue Economy

The World Bank defines the Blue Economy as 'the sustainable use of ocean resources for economic growth, improved livelihoods and jobs, and ocean ecosystem health.' This definition imposes moral responsibility on all industries, especially those that significantly harness or exploit ocean and marine resources in their value chains, to make greater efforts to protect fragile and gradually depleting ocean and marine systems. These have become increasingly susceptible to man-made phenomena, such as ocean pollution, shipping and transport, dredging, offshore drilling, deep-sea mining, overfishing, and the degradation of coastal and marine ecosystems linked to sea-level rise/global warming. Admittedly, tourism-related activities impose significant stress on coastal and marine ecosystems. Thus, the sector must commensurately play a leading global role in adopting and encouraging more sustainable values, attitudes, and practices that will promote healthy ocean and marine systems in the long-run. The role of the tourism sector in promoting ocean health has already been officially recognized in the Sustainable Development Goals (SGDs) by way of SGD 14, which emphasizes a sector's role in the sustainable use of oceans and marine resources.

To ensure that the tourism industry plays its part in contributing to ocean sustainability, there needs to be seriousness of intent, purpose, and action among tourism stakeholders at all levels to address industrial actions that harm ocean and marine resources. Such firm commitment to sustainable behaviours and practices is necessary to help preserve the enormous benefits of healthy marine and coastal ecosystems to the economic livelihoods and survival of billions of people globally. Indeed, oceans cover 70 per cent of the plane, provide us with oxygen and food, regulate the climate, as well as provide habitats for 80 per cent of life on Earth. Overall, healthy marine and coastal ecosystem serve as valuable sources of food, income, trade and shipping, minerals, energy, water supply, recreation, and indeed tourism.

The importance of healthy marine and coastal systems in promoting sustainable tourism is especially worthy of acknowledgement. This is against the background that 80 per cent of tourism occurs along coastal towns and areas while the ocean-related tourism industry grows an estimated US$134 billion per year according to the United Nations Global Compact. The OECD has also predicted that marine and coastal tourism will be the largest sector of the global ocean-based economy by 2030, generating US$777 billion in global revenue and employing 8.6 million people. Small island states are particularly reliant on coastal and marine tourism. It constitutes the largest economic sector for most small island developing states (SIDS) and many coastal states. In the Caribbean, for example, the industry accounts for a quarter of the total economy, and a fifth of all jobs.

Unfortunately, marine and coastal ecosystems are often threatened by tourism development. The areas that attract tourists have been coming under increasing pressure from the damage and pollution caused by tourist facilities and the supporting infrastructure. At the same time, the impacts of climate change, overfishing, and other unsustainable practices, and even some marine tourism activities damage marine ecosystems such as coral reefs that are vital for maintaining ecological diversity and regulating climate. The United Nations has estimated the cost of reduced tourism due to coral bleaching at $12 billion annually. The transition to sustainable ocean economies will, ultimately, require a set of concrete ideas, strategies, toolkits, best practices, and policies that can be standardized and operationalized by all tourism stakeholders working in collaboration with policymakers, regulators, and all other interest groups and stakeholders that are committed to ocean action. The ultimate goal is to ensure that coastal and ocean-based tourism is sustainable, resilient, addresses climate change, reduces pollution, supports ecosystem regeneration and biodiversity conservation, and invests in local jobs and communities.

Resilience is an especially important concept in the context of the blue economy. It refers to the ability of a system, community, individual, or resource to adapt and recover from stress, shock or disruption. In the context of the blue economy, resilience is crucial for the sustainability of ocean resources and the communities that depend on them. As acknowledged, marine ecosystems are under pressure from various stressors, including overfishing, pollution, climate change, ecosystem degradation and habitat destruction. These stressors induce significant economic, social, and environmental impacts, affecting the livelihoods of millions of people around the world. Resilience is, therefore, essential to ensure the long-term sustainability of ocean resources and the communities that depend on them.

While tourism is a key sector of the blue economy, providing economic opportunities for coastal communities and promoting the conservation of marine ecosystems, the industry can also have negative impacts on the environment and the communities it serves, especially areas where resources are limited. Examples include the impacts associated with large cruises, such as the emission of greenhouse gases that contribute to climate change, as well as wastes from ships, which cause pollution and reduce the resilience of marine ecosystems and damage to fragile coastal and marine environment, including corals. Thus, the tourism sector can benefit from resilience by adopting sustainable practices that minimize its impact on the environment and build the capacity of communities to adapt to change. From a post-pandemic perspective, a sustainable blue economy offers a vision for countries' efforts to build back better from the COVID-19 pandemic by shifting away from business as usual and embracing the more sustainable development patterns associated with a blue economy. At the core of the blue economy concept is the de-coupling of socioeconomic development from environmental degradation. The blue economy approach emphasizes the assessment and incorporation of the real value of the natural (blue) capital into all aspects of economic activity – conceptualization, planning, infrastructure development, trade, travel, renewable resource exploitation, energy production/ consumption, etc.

Armed with evidence of the importance of healthy ocean and marine resources to economic livelihoods, biodiversity, and the sustainability of life on earth and below water, as well as the sector's own negative ocean footprints, the tourism industry can start to adopt more informed decisions about the management and conservation of the reefs they depend on – and thus become powerful allies in the conservation movement. Indeed, tourism stakeholders must play their part to promote a sustainable blue economy through raising awareness, establishing behavioural modifications, identifying gaps as well as innovative and scalable solutions. Tourism development in SIDS and coastal regions should consider the potential impact of climate change and global warming and adopt and implement adequate disaster risk reduction policies and practices in order to increase the resilience of tourism sector. Greater attention also needs to be placed on the development of standards for environmental compliance throughout the tourism value chain and systems for monitoring and enforcement. The cruise industry, in particular, needs to continue to accelerate gains in four key areas: controlling emissions, sewage treatment, fuel efficiency, and recycling to reduce it environmental impacts. Overall, the blue economy approach recognizes and places renewed emphasis on the critical need for the international community to address, effectively, the sound management of resources in and beneath international waters by the further development and refinement of international law and ocean governance mechanisms.

It is my view that a blue economy approach, where ecosystem services are properly valued and incorporated into development planning, will further advance the transition of the tourism industry, thereby guiding tourism development and promoting lower-impact activities, such as ecotourism and nature-based tourism, where the natural capital is maintained as an integral part of the process. Finally, efficiency and optimization of resource use are paramount whilst respecting environmental and ecological parameters. This includes sustainable sourcing and usage of local raw materials and utilizing, where feasible, 'blue' low-energy options to realize efficiencies and benefits.

2.

Resilient Tourism for Sustainability

2.1. COVID-19, Geopolitics, and Tourism

By September 2020, there were approximately 30,030,911 coronavirus cases globally and 945,051 deaths. The impact of the pandemic on the global economy to date has been conservatively estimated at $3.8 trillion. During the pandemic, the World Economic Forum projected that the year-end cost of the pandemic would be anywhere between $8.1 and $15.8 trillion globally. The outlook for the global travel and tourism sector was especially bleak as global tourism was projected to lose at least $1.2 trillion, or 1.5 per cent of the global domestic product by year end. International tourist arrivals were expected to decline between 20 and 30 per cent. The tourism sector also faced a staggering one hundred million job losses due to the coronavirus pandemic, according to the World Travel and Tourism Council.

Here in Jamaica, the tourism sector continues to reel from the economic fallout from the pandemic, which significantly reduced arrivals and tourism receipts from major source markets such as the USA, Canada, and the UK. The pandemic derailed preliminary end of year growth projections for the sector. At the end of February 2020, we had recorded a 5.5 per cent increase in tourist arrivals over the same period in 2019. We had welcomed 1.25 million visitors who generated US$859 million dollars in revenues for the country. If that trend held for the rest of the year, we estimated end of year earnings at US$4 billion, with 4.5 million visitors. Obviously, we were forced to revise all preliminary estimates due to the impact of the coronavirus pandemic. The Planning Institute of Jamaica (PIOJ) revealed that of all sectors, tourism suffered the steepest contraction for the April to June quarter because of the sharp decline in stopover and cruise passenger arrivals. From April to August, we welcomed 93,000 visitors, against the original projection of 1.2 million visitors, representing earnings of $4.8 billion and loss of expected visitor expenditure of $53.4 billion, based on originally projected earnings of $58.2 billion for the period. The estimated loss in direct revenue to the government as a result of COVID-19 for the same period was J$19.1 billion. After the border closed in March 2020 most tourism operations ceased, resulting in 90 per cent of the one hundred and seventy thousand persons employed in the sector being sent home. Considering that tourism directly employs 12.6 per cent of the labour force, certainly, this unfortunate development had serious implications for the country's unemployment rate. In spite of it all and against all odds, we, however, weathered and continue to weather the storm.

Tourism has been the most resilient sector of the national economy over the past thirty years, having expanded by 36 per cent against total economy growth of 10 per cent. We have also faced several disruptive events before, from which we emphatically rebounded. For example, the tourism sector grew by 8 per cent in the five years following the SARS threat of 2004. Despite the combined impact of the global financial crisis from 2007 and the HINI outbreak of 2009, tourism arrivals continued to record year-to-year growth; and at the beginning of 2020, the tourism sector was entering its tenth consecutive year of growth. Over this period, the sector has been a catalyst of country's socio-economic progress. Tourism has consistently been the leading generator of foreign exchange, generating up to 50 per cent of total foreign exchange, annually. Tourism drives 15 per cent of construction, 10 per cent of banking and finance, 20 per cent of manufacturing, and 21 per cent of utilities, as well as agriculture and fisheries. The sector contributes directly to 9.5 per cent of GDP and generates approximately three hundred and fifty-four thousand direct, indirect, and induced jobs. Tourism is, undoubtedly, indispensable to the country's macroeconomic stability.

I have also positively observed that many hotels have used the downturn in international tourism as an opportunity to develop special packages to attract locals to their properties. This represents the core objective of the 'Rediscover Jamaica' campaign, which is an initiative launched by The Jamaica Tourist Board to encourage Jamaicans to take advantage of the country's many tourism products and attractions through staycation packages. Taking advantage of rates as low as US$70/US$80 per person all-inclusive, locals have been flocking to hotels for weekends of relaxation. Some hotels have reported up to 50 to 60 per cent occupancy from Jamaican bookers, with some even reporting occupancy as high as 90 per cent during the Independence Holiday period. We are optimistic that this initiative will continue to offset the fallout from decline in international tourism receipts and ensure continued buoyancy of the sector while semblances of normalcy returns. Investors have also continued to show confidence in the Jamaican market and are finishing projects started. I can report that 90 per cent of planned investments for the industry are still on target, despite the effects of the COVID-19 pandemic, thus keeping on track our goal to increase hotel rooms to 25,000 in 2023. A 1,700-room facility will be constructed in St James; 2,000 rooms are planned for Green Island in Hanover, and a tourism development programme for Kingston and Port Royal is also still on.

As a response to the pandemic, we have also made destination security the centrepiece of the recovery plan for the sector. The new-look tourism sector emphasizes destination security through the development and enforcement of rigid health and safety protocols. From as far back as March 2020, when the first wave of the coronavirus was reported in China, measures to be adopted by all tourism entities to prevent the spread of the virus were announced. These measures had three main components; developing the required infrastructure, providing support to the Ministry of Health and educating all stakeholders about the COVID-19 virus. Specially assigned staff members of the Tourism Product Development Company (TPDCo), who are a part of the newly developed Stakeholder Risk Management Unit, closely monitored the implementation of the measures. A COVID-19 coordinator was also assigned to all tourism entities to serve as the point of contact with the Ministry of Health and Wellness and Ministry of Tourism. The coordinator also keeps abreast of health protocols and preventative measures and maintains communication with booking agencies to ensure that information on travel precautionary measures are observed. When the prime minister announced the reopening of the country's borders for international tourism on June 15, we unveiled the Tourism Industry Post COVID-19 Protocol, which was developed to ensure the safety of the workers in the industry, as well as to build confidence among travellers to adapt to 'the new normal' of additional health and hygiene practices. The protocols, which are contained in an eighty-eight-page document, cover all segments of the industry, including airports, cruise ports, accommodations, attractions, tourism transportation operators, craft traders, water sports operators, general security and public safety, and mega events. The COVID-19 Health and Safety Protocols have been endorsed by the World Travel and Tourism Council (WTTC). The protocols have also been globally recognized as providing leadership in tourism COVID-19 management arrangements and having been fully adhered to, have made Jamaica among the most COVID-19-resilient destinations in the world.

We have since created the concept of 'Resilient Corridors' to allow us to manage and trace the movement and activities of tourists along the resort stretch from Negril through Port Antonio on the northern coast of the island. Although only 1 per cent of the population lives along the corridors, they account for 80 per cent of the nation's tourism product. The benefit of the resilient corridors is that they allow the country to tightly manage a small geographic area while ensuring authentic experiences for visitors to the island. The success of our protocols are testament to the high level of compliance by tourism stakeholders, evidenced by the fact that there was no known case of transmission of the COVID-19 within the tourism industry, even as some sections of the island would have reported increased cases. We operated with optimism that our protocols and resilient corridors would boost tourist arrivals, especially from the US based on reports which found that 75 per cent of respondents are more willing to go where they are assured that protocols are being followed.

Ironically, one of the blessings of the pandemic and the period of social distancing is that it unified and brought national stakeholders together in an unprecedented manner to ensure the survival and perseverance of the sector. As attempted to expedite the recovery process, we sought to secure the trust, support, and confidence of sector players and the nation at large. This goal was set to be achieved though the establishment of a team of tourism recovery experts who charted the course for the full reopening of the sector. The team was fit for purpose and reflected an inclusive approach. It comprised nine members, including three industry players and representatives from the Private Sector Organisation of Jamaica (PSOJ), Jamaica Manufacturers and Exporters Association (JMEA), Jamaica Bankers Association (JBA), and the health sector.

On another note, we are very proud of the support that we were able to provide to tourism workers as well as to tourism enterprises during this difficult period through the provision of grant assistance, cash transfer, tax waivers, soft loans, and moratorium on Jamaica Tourist Board (JTB) licenses. We also prepared workers for reintegration into the post-COVID tourism sector by providing eleven free online courses for tourism workers as part of the government's thrust to ensure the continued development of employees in the sector. The courses were offered in areas such as laundry attendant, gift room attendant, kitchen steward/porter, public area sanitation, hospitality team leader, certified banquet server, certified restaurant server, Servsafe training in food safety, certified hospitality supervisor, introduction to Spanish, and disc jock (DJ) certification. Finally, the Tourism Pension Scheme has finally come into fruition. The pension fund has already earned at least $2 million in profit, and we have started to admit persons.

From a geopolitical standpoint, while the long-term implications of the recent global health crisis are yet to be fully measured, we have already observed compelling evidence that a range of economic, political, geographical, and cultural factors have differentiated responses across countries. For one, the COVID-19 pandemic has reinforced the power of the state in its traditional role as protector of society, which sets up a potential situation where the state could assume an expanded world in the post-COVID-19 international system. This would constitute an ideological departure from a recent trend towards a minimal state. Importantly, some of the preeminent global powers struggled with how to balance competing interests at both the national and global levels, including national interests versus global cooperation, rights and freedoms versus public security, individual choice versus consensus-building, economic security versus health security, political/religious ideologies versus science, and idealism versus realism.

Among global powers, there was great anxiety that weakening economies and increased political instability at home would exacerbate vulnerabilities and weaken their power position in global politics relative to their strongest competitors. In particular, it was feared that some global powers would seize the opportunity, in the midst of the crisis, to expand their sphere of influence into then vulnerable territories under the guise of benevolent intervention. Overall, it was generally difficult, or even virtually impossible, for many global leaders to escape the political impact of their policy responses to the pandemic. Key policy decisions had become increasingly subjected to multiple, competing interests which had to be delicately balanced against each other. Undoubtedly, some global leaders faced moral dilemmas in which generally accepted policy responses to the pandemic would have conflicted with narrowed political interests and would have produced sharp ideological contestations among internal groups and with key external actors. Some of the more extreme elements of these ideological contestations have included the proliferation of conspiracy and fringe theories, xenophobic suspicions and fears, widespread perception of attacks on traditional values and freedoms, anti-science sentiments, darwinist ideations, and defiant economic pragmatism.

Universally, two of the most daunting considerations that confronted many global leaders was whether to prioritize the economy or public health or how to balance both. There had obviously been no easy answer to either questions and countries had largely made very calculated decisions where this issue was concerned. Ultimately, all these geopolitical considerations intersected to produce two main consequences: One, the absence of harmonized, universalized protocols for managing the pandemic and two, differences in the success rates of managing the pandemic across countries. Unfortunately, we now live in a hyperconnected world where countries can no longer escape the consequences of the action or inaction of other countries. For their economic survival, some countries were left with little choice but to reopen their borders to facilitate international trade and travel. Of course, questions about premature reopening amid rising infection rates, though valid, were counterweighted against the necessity of economic survival. Once again, this underscores the idea that policymakers were faced with difficult decisions during this period.

The tourism sector is particularly vulnerable to geopolitical factors, as such factors can engender, among potential tourists, an adverse disposition towards international travel, fervent nationalistic values and attitudes, the consequent fear or resentment of other cultures, and increasing insularity or narrowmindedness. Additionally, inefficacy at national levels in managing the pandemic threatened the timely recovery of international tourism or threatened to undo gains made in other countries, especially since many countries with high recovery rates had decided to reopen their borders to international tourists, many of whom would have been travelling from regions with slower rates of success at containment.

Against this backdrop, important questions needed to be considered:

- How will geopolitical developments in major source markets such as the US and China affect the recovery of international tourism?
- Will destination attractiveness and tourist preferences be increasingly shaped by geopolitical considerations in the post-COVID-19 era?
- In light of the fact that tourism is based on the cross-border movements of millions of people, what happens when incompatible geopolitical values and attitudes collide?
- How can small tourism-dependent economies, especially those in the Caribbean that have done fairly well at containing the pandemic, protect themselves from elevated infection risks originating from major source markets without compromising their fragile economies?
- Does the Caribbean now need to look to more geopolitically compatible source markets?
- What will the future of tourism look like for regions such as the Caribbean, Latin America, Africa, and Asia?

The strong evidence of the far-reaching geopolitical impact and consequences of the pandemic necessitates that we deepen our understanding of how emerging or expanded geopolitical considerations are likely to affect the post-COVID-19 world order. The COVID-19 pandemic is perhaps the greatest catastrophic event which we have faced in the modern history of the global economy. Appropriately described as the great equalizer, the pandemic spared no one, as we saw some of the more traditional global powers being stretched to their limits, while, ironically, some of the smaller countries were able to manage the spread of the pandemic with greater efficiency. Irrespective of the sizes and resources of countries, the economic impact of the pandemic has been universal. As the health and human toll grew, the economic damage became evident all around us, and it represented the largest economic shock the world had experienced in decades. It, therefore, became crucial for us to invite national, regional, and global policy-leaders including the World Health Organization (WHO), The United Nations World Trade Organization (UNWTO) among others, to share insights and experiences that would have allowed us to identify and discuss specific geopolitical issues and risks within the context of COVID-19, approaches that could be adopted by destinations to manage these risks, to analyse the particular geopolitical factors that have been indicators or determinants of success in managing the pandemic across countries and to discuss how then current geopolitical developments were likely to reshape in the future.

Tourism in the Caribbean Region

Caribbean island-states are uniquely positioned to benefit from the phenomenal tourism growth that is anticipated to occur globally over the next several years, providing that certain arrangements and strategic planning are put in place on a region-wide basis. As a region, we need to recognize the indispensability of the tourism industry to economic development and act to consolidate and increase shares of the global market. We must also evaluate the existing trends in tourism development that reduce the positive impact of tourism in the region and see how best we can reverse those trends so that tourism, to a greater extent, becomes more beneficial to local economies. For example, despite being the most tourism-dependent region on earth, the Caribbean's share of the global market represents around 2.5 per cent of the 1.2 billion tourism travellers and approximately 3 per cent of global tourism expenditure. The level of tourism dollar retention in the region also ranges between US$0.15 at the low end and US$0.40 at the high end, meaning that tourism consumption by visitors outpaces local production and the host country's capacity to absorb the demand it creates. These negative tourism indicators need to be urgently reversed if the region is serious about promoting tourism as a catalyst for sustainable development in the region. A good starting point in reversing the aforementioned indicators would be for us to carefully examine existing economic linkages, marketing strategies, products and services, policy framework, methods of production, skills set, and application of technology to determine if all these variables are aligned or operate at desirable or optimal levels.

As the region's share of the global tourism market continues to decline and regional economies grow poorer, it has become poignantly clear that the current approach to tourism in the region, defined by insularity, is not capable of promoting sustainable tourism development. Tourism is the region's lifeblood and we can no longer afford to miss tremendous opportunities to improve the sector because of fierce competitiveness, nationalism, and the emphasis on individualism. The time has come for tourism players, within the government and the private sector alike, to achieve some meaningful consensus in developing and implementing a tourism blueprint which establishes a common framework to promote sustainable tourism development in the region. This blueprint should primarily outline strategies, innovations, and policies to be adopted to improve market segmentation, promote product diversification, and to generally enhance the competitiveness and dynamism of regional tourism and deepen the economic linkages between tourism and local communities so that the benefits of tourism development are trickled down to local populations.

The place of tourism in regional economic development has been highly contested. Hoteliers, government policymakers, and tourism-dependent business operators have religiously defended the vitality of the sector to regional economies lauding the sector's tremendous and largely unmatched contribution in individual countries to employment creation and productivity, the growth of the creative and cultural industries, export earnings, foreign-direct investment, foreign exchange, the generation of substantial tax revenues for the government, and the extent to which tourism has supported the growth of other key economic sectors that are linked to it.

On the other hand, a large number of citizens in these countries and many experts in the NGO realm, academia, and economics have relentlessly expressed reservations about tourism's lack of robust economic linkages, largely due to the all-inclusive phenomenon, the dominance of wealth-repatriating MNCs in the sector, low wages being paid to hotel workers, the sector's heavy reliance on imported goods and services, and the sector's negative impact on environmental sustainability. As we move forward, we need to address these broader socio-economic concerns while remaining uncompromised in supporting growth strategies for enhancing the regional tourism product. Indeed, the future of Caribbean economies is hinged on the performance of tourism, and we must find innovative ways of expanding and consolidating economic opportunities from the sector before it is too late. A very good starting point in in this regard would be for regional tourism leaders and pioneers to increase emphasis on building partnerships across the Caribbean archipelago to standardize strategic planning and tourism enhancement activities. One can start by examining the successful regional approach to tourism in the Asia-Pacific region, the lessons learnt from European experiment, and the mysticism of Cuba's re-entry into formal relations with the US, as well as the growing demand among international tourists for value-for-money and dynamic products is an indication that the time is right for the Caribbean to pursue a more aggressive regional approach towards the achievement of sustainable economic growth for our region.

Trends in Tourism Growth in the Region

The only economic sector in the region that has shown relative resilience over the past several decades has been the tourism sector whose importance has grown tremendously in light of the persistent downturn in the other traditional economic sectors - agriculture, manufacturing and mining, especially. Tourism has become increasing indispensable to the economic survival of virtually all Caribbean island-states; and since the 1970s, the sector has been growing at an estimated 5 per cent per annum. Indeed, the region has solidified its position as one of the premier tourist destinations in the world. The contribution of tourism to the growth and expansion of regional economies cuts across all spheres. In fact, the Caribbean is more dependent on tourism than any other region in the world. Tourism is the single largest earner of foreign exchange in sixteen of the twenty-eight countries in the Caribbean. The region has a higher proportion of total employment and percentage of GDP derived from tourism than any other region in the world. It is estimated that one in every four persons is employed by tourism-related activities, and the sector accounts for 41 per cent of all exports and services in the Caribbean and 31 per cent of all gross domestic product.

Tourism statistics compiled by the World Travel and Tourism Council (WTTC) for the year ended December 2014 revealed just how important tourism is to the Caribbean economies. These statistics found that:

- In 2014, tourism directly supported 692,000 jobs (4 per cent of total employment) and over 2 million jobs, directly and indirectly (14 per cent of total employment)
- In terms of the direct contribution of tourism to GDP, the Caribbean (4.5 per cent) ranked third in the world in 2014.
- In terms of the total contribution of tourism to GDP, the Caribbean (14.6 per cent), ranked first in the world in 2014.
- In terms of the total contribution of tourism to employment, the Caribbean ranked first in the world in 2014.
- In terms of contribution to total capital investment, the Caribbean (12.2 per cent) ranked first in the world in 2014.
- In terms of the contribution of tourism to total exports, the Caribbean (17.8 per cent) ranked first in the world in 2014.

Further breakdown of tourism statistics has also shown that five out of the top ten countries and twelve out of the top twenty-five countries in terms of the value added contribution of this industry to total GDP are Caribbean countries. Additionally, twelve out of the twenty-five countries in the world in terms of the average percentage of visitor export receipts in total exports of goods and services from 2006 to 2011 were Caribbean countries. The indirect and induced contributions of tourism to GDP (19 per cent for the region) is almost three times the world average and considerably higher than those of other regions. Annual tourist arrivals for the region have jumped from 11.4 million in 1990 to 28.7 million in 2015, while it was projected for international arrivals to surpass 30 million for the first time in 2016. Considering that the total population of the Caribbean is an estimated 43 million people, these are indeed serious numbers. A few islands such as Grenada, Antigua, Bahamas, St Kitts and Nevis and St Lucia, in fact, had numbers of annual arrivals greater than their populations between 1995 and 2007. Jamaica also registered arrival numbers greater than its population of 2.8 million in 2014 (3.5 million). In 2015, visitors to the Caribbean generated over US$51 billion in revenues and for some island states such as Antigua and Barbuda, The Bahamas,

Barbados, and St Lucia, the arrival expenditure had accounted for about 25 per cent of the total GNI.

Spill over Effects from Tourism

Tourism growth in the Caribbean has had positive spill over effects for the wider economy. Tourism is a broad service sector requiring a wide range of simple and complex goods and services to support it, including the provision of food and beverages, entertainment, transportation, beauty and fashion products, tours, visiting attractions and sites, buying handi-craft and other cultural products, which generally generate economic opportunities in the form of foreign exchange earnings, increased income, employment, and development of infrastructure. Tourism is significantly more labour-intensive when compared to most other industries and, thus, offers greater opportunities for job creation, provides regional policymakers with an opening to focus on positioning tourism to stimulate high-end jobs. A recent development which regional policymakers must seek to maximize is the reopening of the Cuban market to American tourists. The thawing of the relationship between Cuba and the US has resulted in greater number of Americans transiting through other countries like the Bahamas, Jamaica, and the Cayman Islands to visit Cuba. This development should positively impact commerce at airports. Additionally, Caribbean countries must position themselves to absorb the large number of tourists who visited Cuba before the embargo and are likely to be dislocated as hotels in Cuba hike their rates amid an influx in demand.

We need to examine, as possible strategies for enhancing tourism competitiveness in the region, the impact of tourism costs, air connectivity, travel facilitation, and the growing demand for multiple experiences on a single vacation, especially for visitors from far distances such as Asia, South America, Europe, and Africa. Airline costs and the need to secure yield to ensure consistent routes into the Caribbean is a major concern that shared Airlift strategies can overcome. The harmonization of visa policies, airspace usage, and pre clearance arrangements are also useful strategies to consider. Additionally, private sector innovativeness in mergers, acquisitions and co-production in tourism goods and services can increase the production of more indigenous tourism inputs, create jobs, and reduce the leakage of foreign exchange in the region.

The time is right for a tourism summit of ministers and key private sector partners, both within the tourism sector and the supporting sectors, such as agriculture, manufacturing, financial services and utilities, particularly energy, to discuss these issues and develop a strategy for multidestination tourism. Jamaica is offering such a platform and geographic space as we can no longer await solutions from outside the region to rescue our economies, a reality that has eluded us continuously over the years. A start can be made with the countries of the northern or north western Caribbean, including Cuba, Jamaica, the Dominican Republic, Haiti, The Bahamas, Cayman Islands, Belize and the Turks and Caicos islands. The eastern or southeastern Caribbean, including countries such as Trinidad and Tobago, Guyana, and the islands of the Lesser Antilles could engage similarly, thus creating two homogenous zones of tourism collaboration and multidestination experiences for visitors. The urgency and the economic logic which advises this strategy is impatient of time and extended debates. We must act now to secure the economic and human development of our region and secure the real independence of our people.

Certainly, the region can no longer take for granted its coveted position as a premier destination, and calls must be repeated for policymakers to strengthen cooperation aimed at identifying and developing strategies and innovations to consolidate and expand the region's market shares of international visitors and also to make tourism more beneficial to local communities. Tourism remains a sector extremely vulnerable to exogenous shocks, and the region has increasingly faced heightened competition from non-traditional and traditional markets that have begun catering to an increasingly demanding tourist population seeking novelties, value for money, and pleasure maximization that traditional tourism can no longer offer. Only a deeper collaborative approach to tourism development in the region will allow for Caribbean states to combat shared threats and risks and remain globally competitive. Consequently, regional leaders in tourism – hoteliers, government officials, marketers, aviation authorities, etc. – must identify a multidimensional collaborative framework that is best suited for enhancing tourism products and services in the region. Failure to steadfastly and purposefully adopt this collaborative approach may be to the detriment of the long-term competitiveness of our highly tourism-dependent regional economies.

Table 2.1. Tourism vs Other Key Economic Sectors in the Caribbean (as a per cent of GDP)

Countries	Manufacturing	Agriculture	Tourism	Comments
Antigua and Barbuda				Tourism accounts for 69.8 per cent of total employment in the country. It came second in the world (out of 181 countries) in terms of the relative contribution of the industry to the economy, with a 74.9 per cent share of GDP, more than five times the world average of 14 per cent (World Travel and Tourism Council 2011).
The Bahamas	5%	2%	46.2 %	Tourism accounts for 53.8 per cent of total employment in the Bahamas. It placed 9th in the world (out of 181 countries) in terms of the relative contribution of the tourism industry to the economy, with a 46.2 per cent share of GDP, far above the world average of 14 per cent (WTTC 2011).
Barbados	5%	2%	43.5%	Tourism accounts for 42.7 per cent of total employment in Barbados. This placed the country 10th in the world (out of 181 countries) in terms of the relative contribution of the industry to the economy, with a 43.5 per cent share of GDP, vastly above the world average of 14 per cent (WTTC 2011).

Countries	Manufacturing	Agriculture	Tourism	Comments
Dominica	3.5%	13%	32%	Tourism accounts for 29.3 per cent of the total workforce of the country. It ranks 19th out of 181 countries in terms of the relative contribution tourism makes to the national economy, with a 31.8 per cent share of GDP, compared to the world average of 14 per cent (WTTC 2011).
Grenada	4.5%	5%	22.2%	Tourism accounts for 20.4 per cent of the total workforce (World Travel and Tourism Council – WTTC 2011). The country is placed 27th in the world (out of 181 countries), with respect to the industry's relative contribution to the economy, with a share of 22.2 per cent of GDP, compared to a world average of 14 per cent (WTTC 2011).
Guyana	10%	17%	9.2%	Tourism accounts for 8.1 per cent of total employment in the country. The nation placed 86th in the world (out of 181 countries), with respect to the tourism sector's relative contribution to the economy, with a 9.2 per cent share of GDP, compared to the world average of 14 per cent (WTTC 2011).
Jamaica	8.4 %	6 %	7.6%	Tourism directly accounts for 7.2 per cent of the total employment in the country. Jamaica is ranked 26th in the world for the relative contribution of travel and tourism to GDP. This is higher than the world average of 5.2 per cent. Foreign visitor exports account for approximately 47 per cent of total exports (WTTC 2011 estimate).

Countries	Manufacturing	Agriculture	Tourism	Comments
St Kitts and Nevis	5.5 %	2.4%	28%	WTTC estimate that the total contribution to GDP by travel and tourism was 28 per cent in 2011. Consequently, the WTTC positioned St Kitts and Nevis 21st out of 181 countries in relation to relative contribution of tourism to the national economy (GDP), 14 per cent above the world average. Tourism's contribution to the economy is set to rise by 4.7 per cent to 2022. The sector accounts for around 26.4 per cent of total employment.
St Lucia	3.8 %	3.1%	42.5%	The total contribution of travel and tourism to St Lucia's GDP was 42.5 per cent in 2011. As a result of this, the World Travel and Tourism Council estimated that St Lucia ranked 12th out of 181 countries for the relative contribution of tourism to the national economy, above the world average by 28.5 per cent. The sector is a major employer and accounts for over 42.2 per cent of total employment.
St Vincent and the Grenadines	19%	5%	27.3%	The total contribution of the travel and tourism sector in St Vincent and the Grenadines is estimated at 25.3 per cent of GDP in 2011 according to the World Travel and Tourism Council (WTTC). The WTTC ranked the islands 25th in the world in relation to relative contribution of tourism to the economy, 11.3 per cent above the world average. This figure (25.3 per cent of GDP) is forecast to rise steadily over the coming decade. The industry supports 23.0 per cent of total employment.

2.2. New Tourism Model in Post-COVID Era

It is cliché at this point to say that the coronavirus pandemic has decimated international travel and tourism. International arrivals were projected to decline 60 to 80 per cent in 2020; the equivalent of approximately 850 million to 1.1 billion less international travellers for that year. This is in comparison to a 4 per cent decline in international arrivals following the 2008 global economic recession. The labor-intensive sector also haemorrhaged 100 million jobs. The downturn in international tourism continued to present acute repercussions for the global economy well into 2021 and beyond. This is against the backdrop that tourism directly contributes 10 per cent of GDP, generates one in every ten jobs and 28 per cent of global services exports.

For small island developing states (SIDS), where tourism accounts for as much as 80 per cent exports, the impacts of the pandemic have been particularly devastating. Many destinations began to reopen their borders, in a highly regulated manner, with the hope of gradually restoring fluidity to their inbound tourism markets. Some were, however, forced to reintroduce border closures and lockdowns to counter second-waves of outbreaks that had been experienced in some cases. During that time, there was naturally a great (and perhaps unprecedented) sense of paranoia, uncertainty, and anxiety pervading the entire sector and its millions of stakeholders globally. In the midst of adversity, and as they contemplated recovery options, tourism players had to rethink the future of international tourism in an unprecedentedly decisive and urgent manner. Indeed, the changes that have been produced by the coronavirus pandemic have influenced new norms, cultures, expectations, and approaches to enhancing destination security and attractiveness that considerably determine the new dispensation and responses of global tourism in the post-COVID era. Undoubtedly, the post-COVID tourism sector increasingly emphasizes the promotion of sustainability, adaptability, and diversification.

The dominant tourism product that is externally driven, built around laissez-faire tourism behaviours, an over-reliance on traditional markets and that emphasizes quantity over quality has either been replaced or superseded by tourism products designed to ensure the sustainability, adaptability, and diversification (SAD) of destinations. Indeed, the post-COVID tourism sector increasingly takes into account its current and future economic, social, political, and environmental impacts, addressing the needs of visitors, the industry, the environment, and host communities while fortifying its own capacity for risk management and resilience.

The SAD paradigm requires that destinations achieve accelerated segmentation of their markets as narrowmindedness has proven to be a distinct challenge of many tourist destinations. The current hiatus in international tourism flows offers a unique moment to re-evaluate approaches to tourism. One emerging consensus is that tourism may look inwards in the post-COVID era. Many governments around the world prioritized domestic tourism throughout 2020, which meant reconnecting communities and countries with their own culture. As mentioned, in Jamaica, we launched our 'Rediscover Jamaica' campaign to encourage Jamaicans to take advantage of the country's many tourism products and attractions through lower-priced staycation packages based on lower rates. The initiative has received tremendously positive reception from locals, with some hotels reporting 60–80 per cent reservations from locals. As we look to the future, the gap in seasonal downturns in international tourist arrivals and volatility in the global tourism market can be offset by sustaining these staycation packages that target local residents who have traditionally felt excluded from higher-priced all vacation packages designed to attract international tourists.

In the long term, this crisis also presents an opportunity to harness the potential of digitalization to drive new tourism experiences. In the absence of physically travelling experiences, millions of people in quarantine had been seeking out cultural and travel experiences from their homes. Culture proved indispensable during this period, and the demand for virtual access to museums, heritage sites, theatres, and performances reached unprecedented levels according to the UNWTO. Rapid digitalization coupled with emerging technologies, such as virtual and augmented realities, can create new forms of cultural experiences, dissemination, and new business models with market potential. With the lockdown, many public and private providers moved content online for free to keep audiences engaged and satisfy the sharply increased demand for cultural content. New tourist offerings and product should thus be built around creating the digital infrastructure that will allow adventure-minded individuals from around the world to partake in simulated and virtual tourist experiences from the comfort of their homes. In general, the crisis has underscored the necessity for nations to develop tourism frameworks that prioritize the appreciation and preservation of both natural and cultural resources. These models should avoid disturbing the traditions of local communities, ensure the protection of their intangible cultural heritage, and foster an environment conducive to the growth of creativity. It prompted the need for more resilient models of tourism that are in harmony with the environment, safeguarding livelihoods from which local communities benefit.

The post-COVID tourism sector also emphasize health and safety as its cornerstones, as epidemics and pandemics are among the most urgent threats that undermine the future of global tourism. The nature of tourism, defined by cross-border movements and the close interactions of millions, exacerbates the risk of deadly contagions. There is also the view that traditional holiday packages have played into the demand for care-free socializing and indulgences. The COVID-19 pandemic has, however, taught us the importance of considering new business models and product that meet health and safety requirements to build resilience against viral transmissions while remaining attractive to travellers. Moving forward, it is expected that health and wellness will gain increasing priority within the global tourism sector. With the heightened awareness of health and wellness, the demand for more hygiene and sanitation in tourist destinations continues to grow. We have seen more hotels, cruise ships, restaurants, and tour operators upgrade their hygiene and sanitation facilities. We have also seen the revamping of public spaces to allow for physical distancing, the installation of barriers and a move towards touchless technology. Cruise line plans have included temperature checks, medical screenings, testing for the coronavirus, and social distancing protocols. Guests also see more frequent cleaning, transparent shields, abundant hand sanitizers, reminders about distancing, and lobbies reconfigured to create more space. They have also seen limited interaction with workers, as hotels encourage people to check in online and use their phones as room keys.

In this new tourism model, we should also anticipate the growth of smart tourism. The production of visitation data, such as tourists' time spent at attractions, will aid in crowd management – an essential factor in a post-COVID-19 world. Smart tourism aids in promoting social distancing by focusing on controlling human traffic to major tourist sites like a museum, a cathedral, or a public park to maintain the quality of visitors' experiences.

3.
Building Tourism Resilience

3.1. Tourism Resilience Academy

Prior to the COVID-19 pandemic, global travel and tourism experienced ten consecutive year of growth and also outpaced global economic growth for nine consecutive years (UNWTO 2020). International arrivals grew from 25 million in the 1950s to reach 1.5 billion in 2019; representing a 56-fold increase (WEF 2017; UNTWO 2020). For the five-year period preceding the COVID-19 pandemic, the labour-intensive tourism sector supported one in every five jobs created. In 2019 alone, the sector supported 330 million jobs or one in ten jobs globally and contributed US$8.9 trillion to global GDP or 10.3 per cent of GDP; US$1.7 trillion in visitors exports amounting to 6.8 per cent of total exports and 28.3 per cent of global services exports and US$948 billion in capital investment or 4.3 per cent of total investment (UNWTO 2020). The socio-economic impact of travel and tourism considerably varies across regions, with the small undiversified economies of the Pacific, The Indian Ocean, the Atlantic Ocean, the Mediterranean, and the Caribbean being among the world's most tourism-dependent on average.

While travel and tourism has been traditionally considered one of the most resilient segments of the global economy, it is simultaneously and disproportionately prone to shocks. This is as any disruptive event that can reduce inclination to travel and undermine perceptions of destination attractiveness and security. These include natural disasters, climate change impacts, and biodiversity loss, food insecurity, political instability and conflicts, the threat of terror attacks, cybercrime and cybersecurity issues, economic recessions, and indeed epidemics and pandemics. The fallout from the recent crisis has been described as the worst crisis that international tourism has faced since records began in 1950. At the peak of the pandemic in 2020, the sector was set back thirty years, with international arrivals falling by over one billion while global tourism revenues declined by approximately US$1.1 billion over the same period. Similarly, the onset of the pandemic delivered the greatest shock to air travel and the aviation industry since the Second World War as global air transport revenues fell by US$314 billion (-50 per cent) in 2020. The economic cost of the pandemic on international travel and tourism in 2020 further included the loss of approximately 100–120 million jobs and between US$910 million and US$1.1 trillion in export revenues.

The most important lesson learnt from the ongoing crisis is that 'tourism resilience' should no longer be a discussion that is had when stakeholders are frantically contemplating their responses in the aftermath of a disruptive event. There is now an urgent need for 'resilience' and 'sustainability' to be wired into the core of global travel and tourism ecosystems. The tourism sector is one segment of the global economy that is 'too big to fail' and thus can no longer afford to be taken off guard by disruptive events. The sector is now required to take full account of all risks and threats to its competitiveness and develop the necessary toolkits to respond in a forward-thinking, anticipatory, and dynamic manner. This underscores the logic for the establishment of a Tourism Resilience Academy that provides training, toolkits, and curriculum development in tourism resilience studies.

Tourism resilience can be defined as a method to improve sustainability after an ecological or environmental disaster and offers an alternative to sustainable development, as a possible recovery from tourism induced stress. Other interpretations of tourism resilience emphasize the capacity of destinations to not only quickly recover from shocks but to also anticipate these shocks and put in place effective measures and strategies that may either prevent them from happening or mitigate their impact. This reflects the perspective that tourism resilience is an ethos or a core characteristic that should be built into the design of any tourism model. It reflects a proactive approach to assessing, monitoring, and tracking all internal and external risks to the tourism product and building out a robust response architecture. It requires significant investments geared towards resilience-building in areas such as infrastructure development, human resource training, research and development, product diversification and segmentation, risk-mapping, the development of sustainable strategies and policies, leveraging the power of transformative technologies, improving internal and external coordination among stakeholders, the establishment of funding models and insurance schemes, and the establishment of reliable warning systems.

While some threats to the tourism product, especially in the case of the marine-based destinations, have remained largely fixed such as natural disasters (droughts, hurricanes, volcanic eruptions, etc.), cyclical economic shocks and rare global health crises, the past three decades have witnessed the rapid intensification of traditional threats and the emergence of new, aggressive ones. Frequent experiences of political instability and social tensions, infrastructure underdevelopment, and public insecurity in many host regions are negatively affecting perceptions of destination attractiveness and security. Climate change and global warning have resulted in prolonged droughts, more severe hurricanes, and increasingly intractable biodiversity and ecological losses, putting the futures of many tourism-dependent destinations at existential risk. The increasing diffusion of ICTs into the tourism business model, both from the supply-side and the demand-side, has created new, systemic risks linked to cyber-security breaches while the increased pace of international travel in our hyper-connected world exposes destinations disproportionately dependent on international tourists to great biological and epidemiological risks, as evidenced by the last pandemic.

On a more positive note, despite the gargantuan challenges that have confronted the tourism sector between 2020 and 2022, the tireless quest for survival has pushed global stakeholders of tourism at all levels to work together in ways that cut across all pre-existing boundaries and cleavages. Effective leadership within the industry has been central to making tactical adjustments to business operations in the short term to ensure adaptability during the crisis and survival beyond. Many destinations have unveiled a number of action-oriented measures to drive the recovery of the tourism sector. There has been frantic exploration of innovation and creativity to ensure that destinations remain open for business in a safe and healthy environment. There has also been unprecedented attention directed to processes, standards, measurement, and responsible patterns of behaviours by all involved in the value chain to ensure that the sector meets the demands for the delivery of a more sustainable tourism product – one that balances economic, social, environmental, and human interests. Overall, as an unavoidable consequence of the pandemic, stakeholders have also been forced to contemplate, more profoundly, the current challenges and future needs of the tourism industry and how they can respond in a decisive manner.

One positive outcome of this period has been the extent to which destinations have been able to rise to the occasion and demonstrate resilience in the face of extreme adversity. Jamaica's own experience with the resilient corridors has emerged as an example of a disciplined, focused, protocol-based, and data-driven blueprint for safe reopening of the tourism sector. Jamaica's resilient corridors have outperformed many places globally in the fight against the COVID-19 pandemic and have helped to significantly fast-track the pace of recovery of the tourism sector. Globally, the resilience of other destinations has been bolstered by other factors, including strong government response, science and technology, innovation, effective communication, diversification, collaborations, and human capacity-building. Many countries have also developed measures to build a more resilient tourism economy post-COVID-19. These include preparing plans to support the sustainable recovery of tourism, promoting the digital transition and moving to a greener tourism system, and rethinking tourism for the future.

In the final analysis, as global tourism recovers and builds back stronger, having a greater appreciation of resilience is crucial to any successful effort to safeguard the sector from future shocks. The road to recovery as well as the future of tourism crucially depends on the success of the various resilience-building efforts and initiatives being adopted by destinations to respond to the current threats and to prepare for future ones. The notion of a sustainable and resilient tourism requires that the new look tourism industry harmonizes with the environment, promotes the safeguarding of cultural and natural heritage, protects livelihoods, benefits local communities, responds to changing expectations of sustainable behaviours and cultures by all tourism stakeholders. Since 2018, the Global Tourism Resilience and Crisis Management Centre has been at the forefront of building tourism resilience among global destinations. It has become the focal point for developing and coordinating policies, strategies, and interventions to assist destinations in planning, preparing, responding, and recovering quickly from shocks to the sector. One of its thrusts is the continuous engagement of all stakeholders to enhance knowledge and education, to identify solutions, and to build consensus around some of the values and ethos aligned to resilience-building.

3.2. Building Tourism Resilience among African Destinations

As is the case for most other developing regions across the world, travel and tourism has become one of the key drivers of growth across the African continent, especially within the last ten years. In 2018, tourist arrivals among African destinations grew by 5.6 per cent, which was the second-fastest growth rate among all regions and stronger than global average growth of 3.9 per cent. Ten-year statistics for the continent show that tourist arrivals, in fact, increased from 26 million in 2000 to an estimated 70 million in 2019. The contribution of tourism to African GDP was measured at US$168 billion in 2019, equivalent to 7.1 per cent of total GDP. Tourism also generated close to 25 million jobs while visitor expenditures generated US$61.3 billion or 10.4 per cent of total exports. Unfortunately, even against the backdrop of this strong performance among African destinations in recent years, the tourism industry in Africa remains very fragile, simultaneously exemplifying resilience and vulnerability, with both manifesting at regular intervals and with equal intensity.

Despite being the second most populous continent, Africa received only 5 per cent of the 1.1 billion people who travelled to global destinations in 2019. To put this into perspective, the Caribbean, which is a subregion of 43 million people, received 2.8 per cent of the international tourists in 2019, almost equal to Africa's share. Africa's relatively small share of the global tourism market is even more disappointing against the backdrop that the continent is endowed with many natural assets that can enhance its tourism competitiveness, including abundant natural resources, wildlife and marine life, cultural diversity, and extensive natural attractions. The continent thus has great potential to develop certain segments that are growing in demand by international travellers, such as nature/adventure tourism, cultural heritage tourism, and travel for wellness, health, and retirement purposes. We can, however, conclude from the available evidence that the African continent has significant untapped tourism potential. Before African destinations are, however, able to maximize their full growth potential, they will first have to confront some of the major constraints. Africa's ecological and geological characteristics, as well as its geographical location, have been identified as major factors contributing to the volatility of continental tourism. Many African destinations have traditionally, and more intensely since the emergence of the climate change phenomenon, experienced exaggerated risks associated with droughts, earthquakes, floods, cyclones, food insecurity, biodiversity loss, population displacement, and disease outbreaks. Even as countries across the continent are currently battling the fallouts of the COVID-19 pandemic, many are also simultaneously managing other outbreaks linked to cholera, Ebola, Lassa fever, malaria, measles, polio, and yellow fever.

The recent pandemic produced a devastating impact for African destinations. While the case-fatality ratio (CFR) for COVID-19 in Africa remains lower than the global CFR, the continent has traditionally had an underdeveloped and small intercontinental tourism sector, with most of its annual visitors arriving from hard-hit regions and countries such as China, the US, Great Britain, and Germany. Ultimately, the combination of national lockdowns, a tiny local tourism customer base, and an industry aimed at big-spending foreign visitors means that Africa's tourism industry has limited capacity to adapt to prolonged downturn in international travel. Africa recorded a 75 per cent decline in tourist arrivals in 2020 and an estimated US$120 billion in GDP contributions from tourism in 2020. This translates to over five times the loss in receipts recorded in 2009 during the global economic and financial crisis. This also translates into the loss of 12.4 million jobs, or 51 per cent less jobs in the tourism between 2019 and 2020.

Expectedly, many local communities, especially those in the vicinity of wildlife conservation areas which depend on tourism for their economic livelihoods, are now facing risks of starvation and lack of basic humanitarian services due to the steep tourism decline experienced during the pandemic, which also magnified some of the more traditional, structural challenges facing many African destinations. These challenges have weakened their resistance and resilience threshold. They include underdeveloped infrastructure, political instability, lack of security, safety and high crime, difficulty faced by investors in accessing finance, high taxes on tourism investments, low levels of tourism skill, red tape and bureaucracy, and low levels of budgetary support from governments, even in destinations where tourism is a major economic contributor.

Similar to Jamaica and other tourist destinations in the Caribbean, the Pacific, the Atlantic, the Indian Ocean, and the Mediterranean, and South China Seas, many African destinations are also on the frontline of the battle against the twin threat of climate change and global warning and their associated environmental repercussions including prolonged droughts, heat waves, wildfires, rising sea levels, beach erosion, severe storms, floods, biodiversity loss, oceanic acidification, and destruction of vital marine ecosystems. Unfortunately, while Africa contributes the least to global warming, with roughly 2–3 per cent of global emissions, it is the most exposed and vulnerable region to the adverse effects of climate change.

Africa's ecological and geological characteristics, as well as its geographical location, have been identified as major factors contributing to the volatility of continental tourism. Indeed, the risks associated with climate change and global warming are likely to be more economically devastating for the African tourism industry which is predominantly nature-based and revolves around the continent's natural assets such as its wildlife, marine life, natural parks, mountains, sanctuaries, safaris, outback, falls, rivers, oceans, artefacts, and natural landscapes.

Notwithstanding the recognition, however, that a sustainable and healthy natural environment is critical to the attractiveness, appeal, and competitiveness of the tourism industry in Africa, it is equally true that the tourism is both a victim of, and contributor to climate change. Admittedly, the economic livelihoods of many African communities are supported by economic activities that contribute to the intensification of climate change and global warming such as mining, oil production, fishing, forest clearing, hunting and gathering, herding, manufacturing and trading in natural resources. At the same time, rising sea levels, floods, water scarcity, deforestation, biodiversity loss, desertification, wildfires, pollution, drought, and diseases hurt the tourism economy. Unfortunately, like most other developing regions with largely undiversified economies and limited development pathways, African countries are struggling to find solutions that balance social and economic development with environmental sustainability without producing harmful trade-offs or without sacrificing one for the other. Evidently, policymakers face the difficult choice of making these tough decisions that mediate what often appear to be competing, incompatible interests with no apparent optimal course of action.

It must, however, be crucially recognized by African states that economic development and environmental sustainability do not have to be at odds with each other. In fact, they can no longer afford to be at odds with each other. This is considering that failure to reverse the current pace of climate change impacts constitutes an existential threat to many African economies that will exacerbate agricultural decline and food insecurity, thereby threatening the livelihoods of over one hundred million in extreme poverty, adversely impact population health due to heightened risks of transmission of vector-borne diseases linked to warmer temperatures and higher rainfall, likely accelerate the rate of diversion of foreign direct investments (FDIs) for crucial sectors to other developing regions that are viewed as being more environmentally stable and will make African destinations less attractive for international tourists, thereby undermining the enormous economic contribution of tourism especially among countries of eastern, northern, and southern Africa.

It is clear that the task of tourism recovery and building tourism resilience among African destinations requires a strong tourism resilience framework based on elements such as cross-sectorial collaborations, international funding and technical assistance, the development of comprehensive warning systems, the development of resilience barometers, research, and development, human resource development and training, improved marketing tools, greater involvement of the African diaspora globally, building destination attractiveness and security, efforts to build resilience and product development among local communities and also to support the growth of niche markets. As the focal institution for coordinating strategies and interventions to enhance tourism resilience globally, the Global Tourism Resilience and Crisis Management Centre (GTCMC) stands ready to help put together a recovery coalition for African destinations and to enhance the overall resilience of African destinations. This coalition might include African tourism ministers, hoteliers and other industry leaders, the private sector, members of the academic community, members of the African diasporas, community groups, native tribes, and representatives of local, regional, and international tourism organizations. This will build on the work that we have already started through the establishment of one of our satellite centres at Kenyatta University, Kenya in 2019 and another that we have earmarked for Seychelles.

Finally, I also believe that a growing demand for tourism products in the post-COVID era will offer Africa a source of competitive advantage. The demand for tourism products, including cultural, heritage, health and wellness, is likely to grow as visitors' habits increasingly shift from laissez-faire tourism to sustainable tourism. To this end, African destinations in partnership with cruise lines as well as other international tourism authorities, especially in North America and Europe, can explore the possibility of a multidestination arrangements that will allow tourists to, for example, relive the experiences or route of the Middle Passage. African tourism industry leaders should also aggressively target the African diaspora, especially those in the Americas, to encourage them to consider Africa as a viable, attractive tourism market with the goal being to develop attractive products and packages to incentivize diasporic communities in the Americas to visit African destinations.

3.3. Resilience Building for Micro-, Small-, and Medium-Sized Tourism Enterprises (MSMTEs)

The importance of micro-, small- and medium-sized tourism enterprises (SMTEs) to the sustenance and vitality of the tourism sector is an often under-discussed element of our tourism product, but it is crucial that we seriously revisit our strategies for supporting the expansion and improvement of this critical sector of the tourism market. We are well aware that one of the recurring concerns among many Jamaicans is that the tourism sector does not sufficiently support sustainable development and that there is negligible reinvestment of tourism profits into the domestic economy. While the benefits and positive contributions of the tourism sector are well-documented and self-evident, there is also an emerging global view in many parts of the world that the tourism sector has not maximized its potential to fully

visitor experience in areas such as accommodations, restaurants, cultural and creative enterprises, entertainment, attractions and tours, agriculture, manufacturing, foreign exchange trading, duty-free shopping, and other services. The involvement of small- and medium-sized tourism enterprises (SMTEs) and community-based tourism enterprises (CBTEs) should be encouraged as much as possible. They should be encouraged to take advantage of the competitive strengths of small enterprises, for example, in meeting niche markets and specialized goods and services as exists in food and beverage and creative industries.

In many countries, the long-term structural issues of productive capacity and competitiveness of domestic industries require strategies to improve competitiveness, such as identifying suitable niche markets, technology adaptation and innovations, compliance with international standards, reduction and control of production costs and improving marketing information and distribution networks (e.g., through inter-industry consultations, buyer-seller meetings, trade promotion events, and expos). A closer look at our strategic vision for the growth of the tourism sector over the next five years will reveal that the growth of SMTEs will support several of our key objectives such as strengthening linkages with other sectors of the economy, particularly the agricultural and manufacturing sectors, strengthening the benefits derived from the industry by local residents and communities, promoting broader participation by all Jamaicans; and ensuring the safety, security, and sustainability of the natural and built environments. Indeed, our reinvigorated support for SMTEs is aligned with our broader thrust of strengthening current tourism linkages and identifying new areas of potential linkages with a view to maximizing the potential of the tourism sector for generating sustainable economic livelihoods for a larger number of locals, particularly those residing in communities in and around resort areas. For SMTEs to maximize their full potential, we recognize that they will need our help to build their capacities to meet the demands.

Strategies and Initiatives

We have already identified the main challenges facing SMTEs, such as high level of informality, lack of commercial orientation, lack of market information and market access, insufficient access to capital for upgrading, limited customer training, and low ICT diffusion. In Jamaica, the work of some of our agencies, particularly the Tourism Linkages Network (TLN), has been helping SMTEs to overcome some of these challenges. The TLN for example, continues to strengthen and encourage vibrant linkages through several initiatives, focusing primarily on human capacity-building, assisting micro-, small- and medium-sized enterprises with their development, greater integration of local products and services into the tourism product, and expanding the country's potential to tap into new segments of the tourism market. This is evident in the establishment of five networks – Gastronomy, Sports & Entertainment, Health & Wellness, Knowledge and Shopping – to diversify the tourism product, to stimulate increased consumption of local goods; to stimulate entrepreneurship and employment; and to generate and retain more of the country's tourism earnings. We have sought to improve the domestic credit environment for SMTEs through our J$1 billion revolving loan scheme for tourism enterprises.

In 2016, we also initiated the National Community Tourism Portal. This portal has become an excellent marketing tool designed to help local community-based tourism enterprises (CBTEs) keep pace with the competition by building awareness of community tourism in Jamaica, providing comprehensive and engaging information on Jamaica's community tourism product, providing an easy means for making community tourism bookings, and providing CBTEs with affordable and cost-effective e-marketing services. The Tourism Product Development Company (TPDCo) also conducts tourism awareness activities and provides technical assistance on ecotourism, Bed & Breakfast (B&B), agro-tourism, cultural heritage tourism, and arts and crafts development projects. The potential of the craft industry as a driver for growth in the earnings from tourism has long been acknowledged, in spite of its largely informal structure and other challenges to structured development. Five artisan villages are slated to be built across the island. They will be one-stop-shop facilities where visitors can see the creation and merchandising of craft items, while enjoying authentic Jamaican entertainment and leisure activities. It will also provide an avenue for Jamaican artists and craftsmen to expose and express their creativity by producing unique indigenous items, thus, limiting the volume of imported craft items being sold in the industry.

Since the COVID-19 pandemic began in 2020, micro-, small- and medium-sized enterprises globally have been the hardest hit. These enterprises have proven to be the least financially resilient and have struggled to achieve business continuity during a period characterized by changed consumption patterns, demand, product distribution, and consumer behaviours. MSMEs' capacity to adjust to government-imposed restrictive measures has been limited by various factors. These include their challenges in accessing both new and established markets, lower rates of ICT adoption and digital preparedness, limited innovative capabilities, inadequate savings and reserves, high levels of informality with accompanying drawbacks, insufficient ongoing financial backing from the government, debt-related stress, increasing inflation, and restricted storage capabilities. Consequently, many MSMEs globally have suffered significant losses, reduced sales volume, an inability to meet contract terms, a reduction in staff numbers, and have even closed down. The surviving firms must now deal with a changed business landscape in the future, with many patterns of sales, distribution, and consumer behaviour having been substantially and permanently altered. Among MSMEs globally, those operating in the tourism industry have been disproportionately impacted. If you can recall, the onset of the pandemic led to a complete shutdown of the tourism sector. Borders were closed to both air and sea travel, social distancing measures were introduced as well as lockdowns and stay-at-home orders. Most importantly, the large hotels that feed many of the micro-, small- and medium-sized tourism enterprises completely halted commercial operations and have just started to return to pre-pandemic occupancy levels.

These adverse developments have produced several crippling challenges for MSMTEs operating in Jamaica. Many enterprises were entirely dependent on the hotel industry, and its closure immediately resulted in reduced demand, reduced sales, and loss of income for many MSMTEs. Due to the pervasive nature of the economic disruption caused by the pandemic, there was also downturn in demand across the whole economy, which resulted in many MSMTEs experiencing difficulty in identifying new markets outside of the hotel industry. Additionally, many MSMTEs also specialize in the provision of physical goods and services such as craft and handiwork, spa, adventure, transportation, agriculture, manufacturing, and gastronomy, which cannot be provided digitally. Finally, the governments of small states like Jamaica, unlike those of the more developed economies, have been unable to sustain financial support to economic sectors such as MSMTEs due to the increased demand being placed upon limited resources which have been stretched to support interventions in all areas of national life.

Overall, the COVID-19 pandemic has greatly compounded the existing challenges of MSMTEs in Jamaica. While our vast network of MSMTES constitute the backbone of the sector, contributing significantly to the authenticity and quality of the tourism experience, enhancing destination competitiveness and contributing to enhanced brand image, their development has been historically stymied by challenges such as high level of informality, lack of commercial orientation, lack of market information and market access, insufficient access to financial capital, limited customer training, and low ICT diffusion.

Amid the uncertainties that have characterized the current period, an opportunity has, however, been presented for us to rethink strategies for building the resilience of MSMTEs in Jamaica. This requires substantially more coordinated efforts among MSMTEs, tourism authorities, and hoteliers to address market access barriers. Indeed, as we continue to prioritize the plugging of economic leakage from the tourism sector, we must find ways to strengthen the participation of micro-, small- and medium-sized, enterprises in the tourism value chain to ensure that the country can revenue more of its tourism earnings through the increased participation of local entrepreneurs in the sector. This has justified our commitment to establishing stainable linkages between tourism and other productive sectors of the economy to which it is closely linked, such as agriculture and manufacturing.

To bolster our efforts towards this end, the TLN was established in 2013 as an initiative to position the tourism sector to increase its consumption of goods and services that can be competitively sourced in Jamaica. Since its inception, the TLN in partnership with other agencies such as Tourism Enhancement Fund (TEF), Tourism Product Development Company (TPDCo), Jamaica Promotions Corporation (JAMPRO), and the Jamaica Tourist Board (JTB), have introduced a number of initiatives aimed at improving market access for MSMTEs such as the development of the Agri-Linkages Exchange (ALEX) Platform, which leverages the power of technology to connect farmers and buyers in the hotel industry; the annual staging of 'Christmas in July' which facilitates the purchase of authentic local products by stakeholders in the tourism sector and corporate Jamaica looking for gifts for clients and staff.

There is also the staging of the Speed Networking Event, which also connects local producers of goods and services for the tourism industry with buyers to boost consumption of local products and the local economy. Since the launch of the initiative in 2016, over $700 million has been generated in business between local small and medium enterprises. We have also recognized that government support is also crucial in three areas to build the resilience of MSMTEs – training, development, and financing. Training and product development are especially crucial for the delivery of high-quality services by MSMTEs that will that lead to improved visitor satisfaction and enhanced likelihood of return visitors. To this end, our agencies have spearheaded several initiatives. Through the Craft Development Programme, TPDCo has been facilitating several product enhancements, business development, and training programmes, and initiatives to develop the craft industry and diversify Jamaica's tourism offerings. A special Winter Tourist Season Capacity Building Support Programme was also rolled out for the island's craft traders. The initiative provided grants to licensed craft vendors to assist them in preparing for the anticipated influx of tourists during the winter tourist season. The TLN has launched an entrepreneurial training and coaching programme as well as a berry-farming development project geared at preparing farmers to support hoteliers' needs for fresh, high-quality strawberries, raspberries, and blueberries.

Through the recently established 'tourism incubator' initiative, managed by TEF, we also now have a facility in place that supports product and talent development in the tourism sector by nurturing new and start-up enterprises. This initiative provides an outlet for innovative ideas to be developed and converted into material goods that are useful, vital, and authentic. It constitutes a new and exciting dimension of our vision to breed more start-ups, to incentivize knowledge and ideas, and to bring a greater level of innovation in the industry. We continue to target potential stakeholders such as the University of Technology Jamaica, The University of the West Indies (Mona), Jamaica Business Development Corporation (JBDC), and JAMPRO for partnerships to provide grants and loans to support the development and commercialization of ideas generated from the incubator.

We have also recognized that MSMTEs have historically faced constraint in accessing financial capital to undertake the investments that will grow and expand their businesses. The COVID-19 pandemic has further compounded this inherent challenge. From the onset, the immediate response of the government was to provide targeted fiscal support to the network of tourism enterprises, including small hotel operators, attraction companies, tour operators, transportation companies, and entertainment companies, among others. This was made possible through the establishment of $1.2 billion in grants accessible by businesses operating in the tourism and related sectors. This financial support has been backed by other similar financial interventions intended to boost the capacity of MSMTEs to increase their productivity and competitiveness.

The TEF signed a memorandum of understanding with the Jamaica National Small Business Loans Ltd (JNSBL) to make $70 million accessible to operators in the tourism ground transportation subsector who have been negatively impacted by the COVID-19 pandemic. The loans, became accessible at any JN Bank branch from July 1, 2021, and are offered at zero per cent interest rate with an eight-month moratorium on the principal and a maximum repayment period of three years, with no processing fees. The loans can be accessed from Jamaica National Small Business Loans (JNSBL) and will allow borrowers to receive up to a maximum of J$1 million in monthly instalments for up to twelve months. Our latest financial intervention has taken the form of revolving loan facility that has seen the TEF earmarking $1 billion dollars to provide well-needed loans to small- and medium-sized tourism enterprises (SMTEs) to boost the sustainable growth of the industry. The EXIM Bank has been tasked with the responsibility of making disbursements to eligible applicants. Operators in the MSME sector are able to access from a minimum of $5 million up to $25 million at 5 per cent interest for five years. The National Export-Import (EXIM) Bank has, to date, approved and disbursed at least 162 loans valued at some $1.56 billion to seventy-two beneficiaries.

Another thrust of our resilience-building interventions for MSMTEs has been to improve their access to knowledge and information, especially related to disaster risk management, preparedness, and mitigation. This is based on our belief that MSMTES are especially vulnerable to disruptive events, including natural disasters, pandemics, and epidemics and so forth. The COVID-19 pandemic has shown us that they can no longer afford to be taken off guard and instead need to enhance their capacity to anticipate and plan for disruptions. To this end, a part of our efforts to better position tourism enterprises to enhance disaster preparedness has been to produce various disaster risk management tools for our key tourism partners as we seek to implement comprehensive strategies to build resilience within the sector against inevitable disruptions and crises. These include three essential documents prepared by the Ministry of Tourism and the TEF, namely the *Disaster Risk Management Framework for the Tourism Sector, Disaster Risk Management Plan Template and Guidelines for the Tourism Sector,* and *The Business Continuity Plan Guidebook for the Tourism Sector.* The Ministry of Tourism has sought to train tourism stakeholders in using and applying the *Disaster Risk Management Template and Guidelines* and the *BCP Guidebook* to strengthen their own disaster and business continuity plans. Under its Disaster Risk Management (DRM) and Climate Change Adaptation (CCA) programme, the Ministry of Tourism has also sought to develop a framework that mainstreams disaster risk management considerations into the sector's policies, strategies, and plans.

We are also thankful that we now have a think tank based in Jamaica – the Global Tourism Resilience and Crisis Management Centre – with a mandate to assist tourism stakeholders with preparedness, management, and recovery from disruptions and/or crises that impact tourism and threaten economies and livelihoods globally. The centre provides its members with a global network of tourism resilience experts, crisis communication firms, sustainable tourism development professionals, as well as access to an international tourism organization. It also provides access to a global platform to assist with nation branding, global data on tourism trends and changes, opportunities for thought leadership, tourism resilience advocacy resources, and international tourism data.

As we face the post-COVID-19 reality, the ministry continues to strengthen existing partnerships while forging new ones and will also continue to think outside of the box when confronting the long-term challenges facing a crucial segment of our national economy.

3.4. The Role of the Private Sector in Tourism Resilience

The private sector is the backbone of the global tourism industry. While the government's role in the tourism sector is usually limited to policy development, regulation, taxation, and providing a generally enabling environment to support tourism growth, the tourism cycle revolves around the inputs of key stakeholders of the private sector in areas such as marketing, booking, aviation, ground transportation, accommodations, gastronomy, entertainment and recreation, manufacturing, banking and financing, and e-commerce. Thus, undoubtedly, any prolonged disruption to the tourism sector is likely to produce rippled effects for the vast networks of private interests whose economical livelihoods are tied both directly and indirectly to the tourism value chain. The private sector is also a key catalyst of resilience-building efforts in the global tourism industry. Tech companies develop technological innovations to respond to the growing demand for faster information access, communication, and transactions by consumers, as well as advanced cybersecurity toolkits to protect end-users and systems from dangerous cybersecurity threats. Companies are also pioneering a wide range of sustainable and smart products, services, and technologies that are being designed to enhance resource efficiency, reduce the negative environmental footprint of the industry, as well as help the tourism industry to adapt and prepare for the future. Similarly, companies also developed many of the high-tech solutions that have been used to improve screening, detection, tracing, and surveillance during the ongoing COVID-19 pandemic.

Internally, hotel operators play a crucial role in collaborating with policymakers and other key stakeholders to design the policies and strategies that promote resilience and sustainability in the tourism industry. Their role in pursing mutually agreed goals, forging economic links with local sectors, adopting innovative and adaptive technology, and meeting particular health, safety, and environmental standards is crucial to the success of efforts to manage many of the conventional and non-conventional threats facing the global tourism industry such as pandemics and epidemics, cybercrimes, climate change, and high rate of economic leakage. This is also true of aviation and cruise companies as well as operators of tours, adventure and recreational parks. Finally, financial institutions such as banks and insurance companies play an indispensable role in providing funding for resilience-building projects and initiatives, as well as indemnity against many of the more serious risks facing the industry.

4.

Jamaica's Tourism Landscape: A Viable Case

4.1. No Jamaica Without Tourism

Data recently released by the Planning Institute of Jamaica indicated that the Jamaican economy receded by 18 per cent for the April to June 2020 quarter. This precipitous contraction was significantly owed to the estimated 87.5 per cent decline in the hotel and restaurant industries recorded over the same period. Both nationally and globally, tourism suffered the most significant economic fallout as a result of the coronavirus pandemic. Globally, approximately 100 million tourism jobs have been lost. Between March and June, approximately 75 per cent of the total tourism workforce in Jamaica was retrenched, with the remaining 25 per cent working for drastically reduced hours and salaries. For 2020, the country was projected to receive close to three million less visitors than it did in 2019, representing a decline in tourism revenue of approximately US$3 billion. Under such circumstances, the spillover effect of tourism downturn for the wider economy promised to be dire.

Not only does tourism generate direct employment for175,000 Jamaicans and indirect employment for over 354,000 Jamaicans, it also is the single largest contributor to GDP, the main source of foreign revenues, and one of the country's main sources of exports. Tourism also drives 15 per cent of construction, 10 per cent of banking and finance, 20 per cent of manufacturing, and 21 per cent of utilities as well as agriculture and fisheries. Overall, the tourism sector has grown by 36 per cent over the past thirty years against total economy growth of 10 per cent. These statistics indicate the vital importance of tourism to the country's macroeconomic stability. In fact, there cannot be a strong Jamaican economy without a strong tourism sector.

The tourism value chain in Jamaica incorporates many sectors in the economy. Its promotion requires the construction and operation of hotels, restaurants and other tourism related facilities through backwards linkages and the development of basic infrastructure services, such as energy, telecommunications and environmental services, agriculture, manufacturing, and other support services. Tourism also creates a wide range of forward linkages with sectors supplying services consumed by tourists. These include financial, telecommunications, retail, recreational, cultural, personal, hospitality, security, and health services. In addition, to facilitate tourism requires the development of other tourism-supporting infrastructure such as airports, proper roads, ports, hospitals, and banks, which are essential for providing access to high-quality services and creating a competitive tourism destination. All of these tourism-related activities produce positive spill-over effects which cannot be easily quantified.

4.2. Jamaica as a Premier, Luxury Tourism Destination

Jamaica is often conceptualized by many tourists as a luxury destination. It is a representation which manifested during slavery when families and friends visited the island during the cold harsh winter months of Europe, particularly Great Britain. The concept of a luxury destination is often described in the literature of as vague (Stankova and Kaleichev 2013), as 'there is no unified definition for what is luxury tourism as what is considered as luxury depends mostly on the perception of individual' (Koprčina 2020). The idea of luxury tourism usually entails a combination of the following elements: highly-personalized services, high-quality customer service, elegance and flamboyance, authentic gastronomical experiences, cultural authenticity and diverse entertainment products, boutique properties, accommodation with unmatched sophisticated amenities, pristine beaches and landscape, and private utopias for a genuine feeling of intimacy and serenity. Virtually all international destinations seek to position or market themselves as luxury tourist markets that will offer exhilarating and unforgettable products and experiences to visitors. According to a report published by Allied Market Research, the global luxury travel market size was valued at $891 billion in 2018 and is expected to grow at a compound annual growth rate of 7.9 per cent during 2019–2026. During the forecast period (2019–2026), the luxury travel market is projected to be the fastest growing segment of the travel industry worldwide.

The Caribbean region, in general, has become a global leader in tourism, a status that has been largely propelled by the region's natural endowments and its significant investment in building out world-class tourism products. Jamaica, which for many years has retained the coveted status as being the most visited tourist destination among CARICOM countries and the third most visited in the insular Caribbean, has undoubtedly been a standout tourism destination both regionally and globally. Over the years, the island has become the ultimate getaway for many international travellers from North America, Europe, and increasingly Asia and South America. The country's highly diversified tourism product is characterized by the features that contribute to satisfying visitors' experiences mentioned before. Over the years, Jamaica has also copped many other international awards for the excellence of its tourism product. Trip Advisor, the world's largest travel platform, ranked Jamaica the Number One Caribbean destination and the Number 14 Best Destination in the World in 2019. The International Council of the Pacific Area Travel Writers Association (PATWA), which coincidentally is a homophone for the world-famous Jamaican dialect 'patois'), named Jamaica as the 'Destination of the Year' in 2019, while TravAlliance Media named Jamaica the Best Culinary Destination, Best Wedding Destination, and Best Honeymoon Destination over the same period. For fifteen consecutive years, between 2005 and 2020, The World Travel Awards also named Jamaica the Caribbean's Leading Destination, with the country copping twenty-three awards in 2020, including:

- Caribbean's Leading Luxury All Suite Resort (Jamaica Inn)
- Caribbean's Leading Luxury Hotel Villa (Fleming Villa at GoldenEye)
- Caribbean's Leading Luxury Resort (Meliá Braco Village)
- Caribbean's Leading Adventure Tourist Attraction (Dunn's River Falls)
- Caribbean's Leading Villa Resort (Round Hill Hotel & Villas)
- Caribbean's Leading Hotel Residences (The Tryall Club)
- Caribbean's Leading Airport (Sangster International Airport)

- Caribbean's Leading Airport Lounge (Club MoBay at Sangster's International Airport)
- Caribbean's Leading Boutique Resort (GoldenEye)
- Caribbean's Leading Hotel Brand (Sandals Resorts International)

A Snapshot of the Evolution of Tourism in Jamaica

While Jamaica has steadily built out a world class tourism product over the past several decades and currently boasts over thirty-five thousand hotels, accommodations, and condominiums, the evolution of the country's tourism product since the late nineteenth century has been nothing short of remarkable. Given the current gargantuan stature of the country's tourism product, it is hard to imagine that just over fifty years ago, the country only welcomed four hundred and fifteen thousand international visitors, per 1970 figures. This is against the backdrop that, in 2019, Jamaica welcomed over 4.3 million international visitors, who generated over US$3.7 billion in tourism earnings. Nonetheless, even those figures recorded for the year 1970 indicated significant progression of the country's tourism sector since the 1930s. In 1938, the country only welcomed sixty-four thousand international visitors. This figure doubled to one hundred and four thousand by 1952 and exceeded three hundred and forty-five thousand, by 1966.

The Beginning

Overall, the current gargantuan stature of Jamaica as a premier global tourist destination belies the sector's humble, informal beginning. While the net economic impact of tourism in Jamaica today supersedes that of most other sectors, the industry, however, emerged as a 'very informal activity with absentee proprietors and/or wealthy Jamaicans establishing cottages, second homes, holiday homes that provided a place for friends and family to have entertainment and or to enjoy their vacations' (Salmon 2022). Stupart and Shipley (2013) noted that 'starting in the late 17th century, a few wealthy plantation owners with their families and individual travellers vacationed in the island' and that 'such upper-class travel was typical for its time.' Many of the individual travellers to the island were those attempting to escape the cold winters in England and North America

(Gleaner 1995). Kingsbury (2005) also posited that, during the late nineteenth century, Jamaica became an exotic 'Garden of Eden' health resort for rich American tourists who were transported on steamships owned by banana traders from Boston. Factors that aided the initial development of Jamaica as a tourist destination included the island's close proximity to North America and the improvements in transatlantic transportation that augmented opportunities to travel to the region (Martin 1994; Taylor 1993). The first concerted effort to develop a formal tourism industry in Jamaica can, however, be traced back to the year 1890. Specifically, the enactment of the Hotels Law in 1890 was the first major initiative that aimed to offer lucrative incentives to build hotels. The law was passed just in time for the country's hosting of The Jamaica International Exhibition in 1891, which was seen as a potential springboard to launch profitable industries, including tourism (Stupart and Shipley 2013). While, the passing of the Hotels Law in 1890 spurred the development of the industry and saw hotels being constructed in Kingston, Spanish Town, Moneague, Mandeville, and Port Antonio, with the most famous being Titchfield in Port Antonio and Myrtle Bank in Kingston (Salmon 2022), still, annual visitor arrival figures in the nineteenth century were less than one thousand (Taylor 2003). Developments in the early twentieth century would, however, favour the further growth of Jamaica as a tourist destination.

The Second Phase - Post–First World War Surge

In 1910, the Jamaica Tourist Association (JTA) was formed to enhance the attractiveness of the colony as a health and pleasure retreat and to also provide reliable information to both prospective visitors and those already holidaying on the island. The timing of the formation of JTA was ideal since the subsequent events of First World War from 1914–1918 would spur an increased demand for international travel as an outlet for citizens of war-ravaged and war-weary countries of Western Europe and North America to escape their realities. Increased demand for international travel was materialized through improved methods of transportation which facilitated increased cross-border travel (*Gleaner* 1995). Jamaica would attempt to seize this opportunity for tourism growth by establishing in 1922, the Jamaica Tourist Trade Development, the forerunner to the Jamaica Tourist Board, to manage the development of the country's tourism product.

The Third Phase – The Golden Age

By the 1930s, tourist arrivals to Jamaica had begun to show precipitous growth. Annual tourist arrivals moved from roughly one thousand persons in the nineteenth century to few thousands by early 1920s and then to an impressive sixty-four thousand by 1938 (*Gleaner* 1995). The evolution of the country's tourism industry would enter its third and then most prosperous phase in the post–Second World War period. In particular, the 1950s and early '60s was considered 'the golden age' of the tourism development in Jamaica as it was during this period that the country was consolidated as a premier tourist destination in the Caribbean region, after Florida and before Barbados (Butler 1980; Allan 2008). Jamaica's strategic geopolitical importance to the Western Allied Forces of the Second World War (the country was a British colony and Allied base) led to increased aid and infrastructure development. Most notably, a number of famous or wealthy investors started building resorts and second homes on the island, including celebrities such as James Bond creator, Ian Fleming, who wrote about Jamaica's finer qualities; the writer and actor Noël Coward, who was photographed at his Jamaican home for *Life* magazine; and Errol Flynn, the George Clooney of his day (Allan 2008). As the island's fame grew, many other international celebrities would follow suit, including Clark Gable, Charlie Chaplin, Katharine Hepburn, Alec Guinness, Laurence Olivier, and more. The number of hotels constructed in Jamaica would triple between 1945 and 1970. Kingston, Jamaica's capital city, emerged as a jewel in the Caribbean crown, with the construction of large glamorous hotels, downtown cable cars, and a flourishing shopping district (Allan 2008).

To encourage accommodation development, which was in short supply in the 1960s, the Jamaican government offered loans, loan guarantees, and lands to developers through the 1968 Hotel (Incentives) Act. The Act was designed to increase the island's accommodation capacity and position tourism as an engine of rural development. The Act facilitated a 'tax holiday' of 10 to 15 years for approved hotels, based on location. It also lifted duty on all imported materials and equipment (Stupart and Shipley 2013). Owing to these developments of the 1950s and '60s, in 1952, the number of tourist arrivals had reached over one hundred and four thousand

(*Gleaner* 1995). Tourist arrivals subsequently moved from 191,303 in 1954 to 396,347 in 1968, while tourists' expenditure moved from US$28 million to US$87.8 million during the same period (Martin 1994). During this period, it was noted by Taylor (1993) that accommodation had a hard time catching up with demand, although the number of beds increased from 5,800 in 1959 to 8,413 in 1969. The consolidation of Jamaica as an important tourist destination during this period was chiefly facilitated by a number of factors, including the opening of new commercial jet routes, first from Miami then direct from New York and London; the influx of foreign capital which led to more accommodations and restaurants, even in the now-crime-crippled capital; accommodations and restaurants, even in the now-crime-crippled capital; the rapid growth in disposable income in North America; the Cuban Revolution of 1959, and the subsequent US embargo that included the suspension of travel by US citizens to the island; the introduction in 1969 of a national airline, Air Jamaica; and tax incentives and duty-free imports of building materials and equipment for hotels (Martin 1994; Henry 1987). By the mid-1950s, Jamaica was being serviced by eight international airlines including BOAC, BWIA, PAA, SKLAM, TransCanadian Airways, Delta, Avianca, and Avenca.

The Emergence of The 'All Inclusive' Concept

It was also during the 1950s that the all-inclusive concept became adopted in Jamaica. The evolution of Jamaica as a world-renown luxury tourism destination is significantly owed to the vision of one man, hotel industry pioneer and father of Jamaican tourism, Abraham 'Abe' Issa, who conceptualized the all-inclusive concept in 1949, with the opening of the country's first all-season resort. Following its opening in 1949, the Tower Isle Hotel quickly rose to fame, attracting Hollywood stars, sporting legends, and even British royalty. In 1955, Issa was appointed president of the newly created Jamaica Tourist Board. He embarked on an aggressive marketing campaign, both locally and internationally. The advertising and publicity Issa generated for the hotel industry was hugely successful. Under his direction, the number of tourists arriving on the island almost tripled between 1955 and 1962. The all-inclusive business model has come to define Jamaica's tourism sector.

The 1970s and '80s – From Downturn to Resurgence

After a twenty-year period of growth, the tourism industry would suffer a steep downturn in the mid-1970s due to changes in domestic policies under the democratic socialist regime of Michael Manley and the consequences of retaliative foreign policy responses of Western governments, especially the US. The radical policy shift of the Jamaican government, which resulted in deeper political alignment with USSR and the Cuban communist model and ultimately impaired relations with the country's traditional Western allies, contributed to negative international press, high rates of out-migration, and the eventual deterrence and flight of needed capital, business interests, and tourists (Allan 2008). The downturn of the 1970s was, however, quickly reversed in the 1980s, following the decision of the newly elected government to restore full diplomatic and economic relations with the country's traditional Western allies and embark on a programme of economic liberalization that positioned the country favourably to attract high levels of foreign direct investment and to recapture its mass tourism appeal.

In the 1980s, the government divested numerous hotels that were purchased by the government in the 1970s. The increased foreign direct investment in tourism that resulted from this move resulted in the country's room stock growing to more than eleven thousand rooms, complemented by over seven hundred hotels and various other guest houses. Data indicate that net earnings from tourism nearly doubled in the first six years of the 1980s, reaching US$437 million in 1986. Tourist arrivals increased 53 per cent over the five-year period from 1981 to 1985, while hotel occupancy rates rose from 41.5 per cent in 1981 to the 70 per cent range in 1986 and early 1987. Direct employment in tourist hotels also increased from 9,527 in 1980 to 13,619 in 1985. By the end of the 1980s, Jamaica ranked second only to the Bahamas as the preferred vacation location for American tourists in the Caribbean.

The 1990s and 2000s – Era of Mega Hotel Development

Since the 1987–88 season, the number of annual tourist arrivals to Jamaica has exceeded one million and has continued to grow, driven significantly by steep increase in cruise passenger arrivals (*Gleaner*

1995). The 1990s into 2000s has been characterized by a strong wave of hotel development, with a surge in Spanish investments, some of which have resulted in mega hotel construction exceeding five hundred rooms and, in some instances, one thousand rooms (Salmon 2022). As a result of the explosion in mega hotel construction, data indicate that the number of beds in the accommodation subsector increased from 8,413 beds in 1969 to seventeen thousand in 1979 to over sixty thousand in 2009 (Stupart and Shipley 2013). The country's hotel-room count increased by 123 per cent between 1986 and 2006, reaching 19, 550 in 2006 (Jamaica Information Service 2007). Today, the country's hotel room stock is estimated at thirty-three thousand with a projection for twelve thousand new rooms to be added by 2025 (Morris 2019).

Current Economic Impact

Equally, the economic contributions of tourism in Jamaica have grown precipitously since the 1990s. Gross foreign exchange generated by tourism has moved from over US$100,000 per year in the 1950s to US$740,000 in 1990 to US$1.3 million in 2000 to US$1.6 billion in 2010 to a record high of US$3.7 billion in 2019. It is anticipated that the country will exceed US$5 billion in earnings for the 2023 calendar year, based on the current trend in the industry's out-turns.

Figure 4.2: Tourist Arrival Figures from 1930s to 2000s (Selected Years)

Year	Tourist Arrivals	Year	Tourist Arrivals
1938	64,0000	**1995**	1,752,000
1952	104,000	**2000**	2,230,000
1954	191,303	**2005**	3,016,000
1966	345,000	**2010**	2,832,000
1968	396,347	**2015**	3,692,000
1970	415,000	**2019**	4,233,000
1985	846,716		

Statistics produced by the Caribbean Tourism Organization (CTO) also indicate that the period 1991–2000 was marked by a consistent uptick in tax revenue from tourism in Jamaica. In 1991, tax revenue to the government totalled US$532, 200 million. At the end of 2000, the government earned US$1,977,900 million (Johnson 2014). The country is also expected to welcome five million visitors in 2024, one year ahead of the earmarked timeline.

Jamaica's Tourism Product Today

Today, the nation boasts some of the most exquisite offerings in luxury tourism. Each year, over three million tourists visit the island. Luxury travellers have an array of choices, ranging from lavish resorts and captivating attractions. These options encompass Trident, Geejam, and Dragon Bay Resort nestled in the verdant parish of Portland. Adjacent in the neighbouring parish of St Mary, one can discover Golden Eye, Couples Tower Isle, and Couples Sans Souci. In the world-famous Ocho Rios, there is Dunn's River, the Bahia Principe, Moon Palace Jamaica All-Inclusive Resort, Sandals Ocho Rios, Sandals Royal Plantation, Jamaica Inn, and Hotel Riu. Trelawny offers venues like Royalton White Sands, Royalton Blue Sands, and Melia Braco Village. In Trelawny, one can also indulge in The Grand Palladium and The Tryall Club, while Montego Bay boasts The Half Moon Hotel, Round Hill, Hilton Rose Hall, Secrets Wild Orchid, Iberostar, Zoetry, Hyatt Ziva, Breathless Resort, S Hotel, and Sandals Royal Caribbean. Negril presents The Caves, Tensing Pen, Ricks Café, Couples Swept Away, Royalton Negril, and Hedonism II. The recent entry of luxury groups in the market such as Hard Rock, Margaritaville, and Nickelodeon by Karisma Hotels & Resorts, Panama Jack by Playa Hotels & Resorts will certainly broaden the options available to visitors and help to enhance the country's product offerings.

Outside of these spectacular accommodations, the island offers excellent facilities for tennis, golf, and equestrian sports. Water sports of all sorts are available. Jamaica has plantation tours and great houses, dolphin parks and nature reserves, museums, galleries and soft adventure tours. There are also numerous craft markets and duty-free stores for goods, both bargain and luxury. The island's cuisine has been shaped by the people who have made Jamaica their home. Jamaica has many fine restaurants which offer an array of dining styles in Jamaican, American, Continental, East Indian, Chinese, and Italian cuisines, among others. There is also a wide variety of festivals and entertainment events year-round, including community and international festivals. Jamaica's native music – reggae – is celebrated in many festivals including Reggae Sumfest, Reggae Sunsplash, and Rebel Salute. For international travellers who are truly interested in creating once-in-a-lifetime magical experiences, visiting this piece of heaven on Earth called Jamaica must be on your bucket lists.

5.

Advancing Tourism in the Digital Landscape

5.1. Tourism and the Digital Landscape Post-COVID

Undoubtedly, the ubiquitous disruptions caused by the COVID-19 pandemic has dramatically accelerated the pace of digital transformation. All across the world, the adoption of stay-at-home and work-from-home orders, border closures, and other strict social distancing measures to manage the pandemic undermined traditional systems and processes, resulting in most major government, commercial, and work-related activities being migrated to digital channels. In the process, the attitude of policymakers, organizations, and even members of the public towards digital technology has shifted from scepticism, uncertainty, and ambivalence to a firm acknowledgment that digital technology now constitutes an important catalyst of social and economic development. Importantly, the pandemic has taught us that organizations that fail to successfully incorporate digital technologies into their business models will likely fail in their quest to ensure adaptability, agility, and competitiveness in the post-COVID era.

The ability of players in the global tourism sector to adapt to the impact of the pandemic has been undoubtedly aided by digital technologies. In general, robotics, artificial intelligence, and human-robot interactions would have been increasingly deployed to manage the spread of COVID-19 in hospitals, airports, transportation systems, recreation and scenic areas, hotels, restaurants, and communities in general. Humanoid robots, autonomous vehicles, drones, and other intelligent robots are used in many different ways to reduce human-to-human interaction and to provide personalized, responsive services.

Travel, tourism, and hospitality, in particular, were disproportionately impacted by the lockdowns used to maintain social distance to manage the pandemic. Information and communications technology (ICTs) would have shown considerable potential to improve the delivery of critical information services in the tourism industry during this period. Since the pandemic began, travel and tourism enterprises across the world began leveraging ICTs to improve almost all areas of the hospitality industry, such as guest services, reservations, food and beverage management, sales, food service catering, maintenance, security, and hospitality accounting. They rolled out a number of information-based digital innovations to facilitate service-delivery in a quick, convenient, and safe manner. These include using mobile apps to enable customers to book reservations, check-in, order and pay for services using their devices, using digital workforce, including chatbots that provide pre-determined answers to frequently-asked questions (FAQs) and live chat with on-property staff, and using digital keys through in-app features that enable guests to unlock their hotel rooms by tapping their mobile devices. As customers are demanding faster response times on online platforms, artificial intelligence has allowed businesses to deliver efficiency that would be impossible for humans. For example, chatbots are now able to respond to questions and provide valuable information to customers, even when a customer service representative is not available. Chatbots used by two hotel chains in Singapore are even able to conduct health declarations, facilitate contactless ordering for dine-in services, and manage crowd control. Cloud-based IoT (Internet of Things) software can also now be used to manage back-of-house functions and streamline operational complexities like coordinating housekeeping systems, assigning staff duties, and confirming compliance with newly enhanced cleanliness standards.

Generally, AI-enabled technologies are increasingly being used in the tourism industry to improve personalization, tailor recommendations, and guarantee fast response times, even in the absence of staff. From tangible restaurant menus and paper in-room compendiums with scannable QR codes to contactless hotel check-in capabilities, mobile room keys, touchless payments, and in-app ordering, and appointments-booking, almost every aspect of the hospitality experience can now be accessed through guests' own mobile devices, provided that hotels have adopted the right software. Robotics have also grown increasingly more important in hospitality and tourism-industry settings to provide concierge, housekeeping, food, and other service tasks. From preparing food and beverage in room dining services, doubling as waiters in hotel restaurants, delivering housekeeping items, dispensing facemasks and hand sanitizers, robots are used on the frontline to protect hotel guests and employees and prevent the spread of COVID-19. In South Korea, bots have been delivering water bottles, fresh towels, and other amenities to guests.

In the absence of physical travel, millions of people in quarantine have also been seeking out cultural and travel experiences from their homes. With local tourism attractions looking to minimize contact and leverage technology for social distancing, the digital space is tapping into augmented and virtual realities to provide simulated visits to different places and famous landmarks. This is as the demand for virtual access to museums, heritage sites, theatres, and performances has reached unprecedented levels according to the United Nations World Tourism Organization.

So, as we manoeuvre the post-COVID period, digital technologies have become important catalysts of ensuring both economical and sustainable pathways for the tourism sector moving forward. The combination of cutting-edge technologies offers solutions to current challenges and can help revive the hospitality sector in a period when touch-free or contactless solutions have become the norm. AI and smart technologies can be leveraged to quickly rewire the current physical interfaces to touch-free, gesture-based, or voice-activated interfaces. Consequently, artificial intelligence is increasingly being used to enhance a plethora of services in the hotel industry, including fleet and operations management, disruption management, customer service and retention, and autonomous machines and services. Overall, the trend towards a digital marketplace in the tourism sector is also poised to intensify post-COVID-19. Most travel and tourism-related business, including destination research, booking and paying for experiences during a vacation are done virtually. The trend thus instructs all tourism enterprises, micro-, small-, medium-sized and large, to find ways to embrace digital technologies and develop their digital architectures or face the risk of being left behind.

5.2. Tech Beach Innovation and Tourism

The world has entered the Fourth Industrial Revolution. This constitutes a new chapter in human development, enabled by extraordinary technology advances, including the rapid development and diffusion of innovations, the fusion of the digital, biological, and physical worlds, as well as the accelerated utilization of new technologies, such as artificial intelligence, cloud computing, robotics, 3D printing, the Internet of Things, and advanced wireless technologies, among others. These technologies are changing the way, individuals, businesses, and governments operate and interact, which is producing a total transformation of society, similar to, but more disruptive, than the changes produced by previous industrial revolutions.

This increased availability and use of digital technologies present an opportunity for policymakers to work with other stakeholders to swiftly adopt holistic long-term strategies for ICT development and lead in adapting governance and leadership behaviours to ensure that ICTs deliver maximum benefits. Indeed, both the private sector and governments need to increase investments in innovative digital solutions to drive social impact.

Travel, tourism, and hospitality, in particular, has been disproportionately impacted by the lockdowns used to maintain social distance to manage the pandemic. The adoption of digital solutions and innovations has the potential to provide both economic and sustainable pathways for the travel sector moving forward. The combination of cutting-edge technologies offers solutions to current challenges and has helped to revive the hospitality sector in a period when touch-free or contactless solutions have become the order of the day. When tourism enterprises around the world began to reopen, fewer resources were available, and a new operating model to minimize contact was considered and deployed. Fortunately, a range of innovations can be leveraged to quickly rewire the current physical interfaces to touch-free, gesture-based, or voice-activated interfaces. Ultimately, digital innovations can be used to enhance a plethora of services in the hotel industry, including fleet and operations management, disruption management, customer service and retention, and autonomous machines and services.

Digital innovations also offer solutions to challenges facing the travel industry by helping to reduce pressure on staff while adhering to safety-guidelines, loyalty-tiers, and personal preferences. Next generation predictive analytics services and solutions harness the power of big data to advise pilots of efficient ways to fly, change the way travellers board aircrafts, and to reduce energy consumption. As tourism minister of a tourism-dependent nation, my ministry and its agencies have made innovation an important element of our agenda to enhance tourism competitiveness and reform in Jamaica. We have introduced applications that have made it easier for local producers to market and distribute their products and increase their customer base while at the same time making it easier for stakeholders to access market and management data, to share information, and build trading partnerships. Overall, the adoption of online market information platforms has helped local producers to access centralized information about organizations, production nodes, and business information that may help them to make more informed decisions on investment or identify new suppliers or customers.

At the height of the pandemic, the ministry and its agencies also found creative ways to adjust to sharply declined international tourist arrivals. When most international borders closed, the Jamaica Tourism Board quickly sprang into action by developing a number of campaigns and digital content series. We introduced Virtual *Tours of Jamaica* as a content series that provides visual inspiration to travellers to add Jamaica to their itineraries by showing short tours of destination hotspots such as Dunn's River Falls, Blue Lagoon in Portland, 7 Mile Beach in Negril, Exploring Montego Bay, and the Rustic Luxury of the South Coast. The JTB also added a new and exciting feature to its visitjamaica.com platform, with the launch of the 'My Heartbeats JA' microsite, which allows visitors to book their wedding, honeymoon, or romantic getaways. The country's strong presence in the virtual marketplace was affirmed by the fact that local hotel properties executed over one hundred virtual weddings while last year's staging on Jamaica Product Exchange (JAPEX), made possible through weekly destination webinars hosted by JTB Regional Sales Teams, was the largest in history. In spite of the challenges, we also forged ahead and hosted other signature events in 2020, such as the *Christmas in July Trade Show*, *Style Jamaica Shopping Showcase*, the *Jamaica Blue Mountain*

Coffee Festival, *Jamaica Health and Wellness Tourism Conference*, *Spa Standards Sensitization Workshops*, the *Jamaica Rum Festival*, and our *Speed Networking event* – using virtual formats. The Linkages Network also hosted a successful virtual Gastronomy Forum series to prepare the culinary industry for the rebound of the tourism sector. The series included presentations on innovation in gastronomy; developing destination restaurants; social media and digital marketing, as well as talent development

In the final analysis, those in the travel and hotel industry who use technologies to help customers through these difficulties are likely to bounce back more quickly and see their customers return. Not only can AI increase demand, adapt at speeds faster than human counterparts, and drive revenue, but it can also be deployed to save businesses considerable financial losses and aid them in manipulating the 'new normal' that defines the post-COVID tourism industry.

5.3. Tourism and Multidestination

The question of tourism sustainability and competitiveness is especially urgent for tourism-dependent small island dependent states, like those in the Caribbean, that are acutely vulnerable to disruptive events. Tourism is the single largest generator of foreign exchange in sixteen of the twenty-eight countries in the Caribbean and also the sector receiving the most FDI. The region has a higher proportion of total employment and percentage of GDP derived from tourism than any other region in the world. These data point to the enormous importance of rethinking and restructuring the tourism value chain in the Caribbean to ensure that the industry's economic benefits can be spread more widely across the whole region.

One of the drivers of tourism competitiveness is the ability of destinations to develop more tourism products and packages that satisfy the growing need of international travellers for diverse, authentic, and gratifying experiences. Thus, the enhanced competitiveness of Caribbean tourism will require more collaborative strategies among regional stakeholders to co-develop products and offerings to attract new markets. Notably, international travellers have become far more demanding and have higher expectations of the destinations to which they travel or intend to travel. International tourism trends are showing a shift from the traditional 'sun, sea and sand' towards interactive experiential tourism. Indeed, International tourists want to maximize their travel experiences by exploring as many sites, attractions, and locales as possible. One way to satisfy this demand is greater focus on the development of multidestination arrangements.

Regionalism has been long established as a viable framework for promoting integration and cooperation in trade and other areas to enhance the region's competitiveness, deepen its integration into the global economy and address major socio-economic problems such as poverty and unemployment. A large market created by integration can promote economies of scale, sharing of economic costs and benefits, knowledge and skill transfer, and the pooling of resources to meet common goals for effectively tackling shared challenges and risks. Tourism has been identified as one of the sectors that enjoy enormous potential to promote regional integration.

It has already been recognized that the future fortunes of Caribbean tourism may lie in economic convergence between complimentary economies. Against this backdrop, multidestination arrangements can increase intra-regional tourist flows and promote mutual benefits for more destinations in the region. The multidestination strategy is one of three legacy outcomes from the United Nations World Tourism Organization (UNWTO) in 2017. A multidestination arrangement is based on joint partnerships involving governments airlines, hotels, tour operators, and attractions that will enable visitors to seamlessly travel two, three, or more geographically proximate nations and stay over in each destination. The countries of the north-western and south-eastern Caribbean are well positioned to embrace this new architecture as their geographic alignments are clear and are all within an hour-and-a-half by air or sea from each other, making it easy for island-hopping and experiential enrichment for the visitor.

The value of a multidestination arrangement is that, as an approach to tourism development, it adds value to the tourism experience, while expanding the benefits of tourism to more than one destination. In this regard, multidestination tourism can be considered one of the complementary means to diversify the regional tourism industry while capitalizing on the region's unique natural and cultural assets and contributing to social and economic growth. From a visitor's perspective, a multidestination tourism package will afford the opportunity to experience different destinations/localities, with each experience fulfilling a different desire or interest. Several regions have already started exploring the feasibility of multidestination arrangements. Government agencies, tourism boards and private companies from seven countries in Central America have launched a joint partnership to promote multidestination travel in the region, offering travel packages at special rates. Eight packages are being promoted, and tours include destinations in two, three, or even all seven countries. Options include offers to enjoy, for example, ecotourism in Costa Rica, culture in Guatemala, and beach destinations along the Caribbean coastline in Honduras. Similarly, Jamaica currently has four multidestination arrangements with the government of Cuba, the Dominican Republic, and Panama and another in the pipeline with the government of the Cayman Islands.

These multidestination arrangements are aimed at advancing regional integration by fostering and harmonizing legislation on air connectivity, visa facilitation, product development, marketing, and human capital development. The convergence of the five countries has also created a market of over sixty million potential visitors and has been promoted as a package, through the respective tourist boards, to large tour operators, airlines, and cruise lines. This constitutes a major development for tourism's growth and expansion in the Caribbean area, as it has brought five of the largest markets in the region together. The agreements have created a mega-market that will now be able to attract the big airlines, the large tour operators but more importantly destinations will now be able to entice the new emerging markets of the far distances of Asia, Africa, and Eastern Europe.

In spite of its potential benefits from a regional perspective, some prerequisites have to be met for the successful implementation of multidestination arrangements. Governments need to work closely to examine the issues of tourism costs, air connectivity, the harmonization of visa policies, airspace usage, and pre-clearance arrangements. One possibility that can be effectively explored is adopting measures that would enable tourists to travel more conveniently to and among the countries of the region, such as visa waivers for select countries or a multiple-entry visa. There should also be willingness and commitment on the part of the countries to coordinate marketing, product development, and investment strategies. Governments are also urged to explore incentives and strategies to strengthen regional carriers, enhance intra-regional travel, and through joint airlift agreements, increase linkages between regional and international airlines as part of a broad-based strategy to boost tourist arrivals.

6.

International Trade and Tourism

6.1. Regional Integration and Tourism

The Caribbean region is paradoxical. The region's closeness to major trading markets, its tropical climate, its valuable natural and cultural resources, and its high rate of human development are well-established sources of competitiveness in global trade and catalysts for attracting investments. Nonetheless the region's development has been constrained by a number of factors, including the small size of islands, environmental vulnerability, and insufficient economic integration among countries. For these reasons, among others, deepened regional integration is critical for promoting the sustainable development of Caribbean states.

Regionalism has been long established as a viable framework for promoting integration and cooperation in trade and other areas to enhance the region's competitiveness, deepen its integration into the global economy, and address major socio-economic problems, such as poverty and unemployment. A large market created by integration can promote economies of scale, sharing of economic costs and benefits, knowledge and skill transfer, and the pooling of resources to meet common goals for effectively tackling shared challenges and risks.

At the 39th CARICOM Heads of Government meeting held in Montego Bay, regional leaders in attendance reaffirmed their commitment to the effective implementation of the CARICOM Single Market and Economy (CSME) to ensure that the initiative meets its main objective of facilitating the expansion of investment and trade in goods and services, as well as the free movement of people across the region. The need to deepen economic integration with other non- CARICOM states such as Cuba and the Dominican Republic was also discussed. Tourism has been identified as one of the sectors which enjoy enormous potential to promote regional integration. Tourism shares a special place among Caribbean states being a shared model of development for the region. Regional leaders at the 29th Inter-Sessional Meeting of the Conference of Heads of Government of the Caribbean Community (CARICOM) held at Port-au-Prince, Haiti, from February 26–27, 2018, acknowledged tourism as the Caribbean's largest economic sector and declared that the sector needs to be 'stimulated urgently and sustainably for the region's long term development prospects.'

The Caribbean is the most tourism-dependent region in the world. The sector generates investments and jobs for all the islands and supports overall economic growth through critical sectorial linkages. The tourism sector, by its very nature, also promotes some of the main values of regional integration as tourism involves the close contact and interaction of millions of individuals from diverse cultural, ethnic, racial, socio-economic, and national backgrounds working together for mutually beneficial exchanges. The tourism sector is also multidimensional, cutting across many spheres, sectors, and boundaries. The sector thus provides considerable scope for collaboration and cooperation among many stakeholders at the regional level in a wide range of areas, including investment and product development, human resource development, tourism awareness, research and statistics, access and transportation, regional facilitation, environmental and cultural sustainability, marketing communications, and addressing crime that involves visitors.

It is no secret that there remains several impediments to the development of a sustainable regional tourism sector, including the general lack of emphasis and promotion of intra-regional tourism at national levels, the prohibitive cost of intra-regional travel, continued restrictions to free movement, and insufficient harmonization and coordination in the area of disaster risk management. The shared vulnerabilities and threats to the tourism sector in the region presented by climate change and other issues necessitate sophisticated resilience mechanisms and crisis management systems. These threats have heightened the need for Caribbean countries to deepen cooperation and coordination in the security sector in order to create a favourable environment for tourism development. Increasingly, the harmonization and standardization of disaster preparedness and emergency response systems across Caribbean countries in areas such as laws and regulations, increasing intelligence and information-sharing, surveillance and detection, and capacity-building has become the main strategy for enhancing the capacity of the region to respond to major threats such as climate change, epidemics and pandemics, terrorism, and cybercrimes. Indeed, it was this spirit of regional cooperation that led to the recent conceptualization of the Caribbean Disaster Resilience Centre, the first of its kind in the region, to be established at The University of the West Indies, Mona.

The Caribbean Disaster Resilience Centre is tasked with creating, producing, and generating toolkits, guidelines, and policies to handle the recovery process from the minute a crisis takes place. The centre is aimed at enhancing regional capacity to manage a range of chronic challenges that can be destabilizing to our societies. Ultimately, tourism cooperation can create a combined political will that provides security and safety for international tourists and nationals alike.

Tourism is also a catalyst for promoting the successful implementation of the CSME framework which has been the leading initiative developed by CARICOM to promote regional integration. With respect to tourism in particular, the relevant components of the CSME include the free movement of tourism professionals (skilled persons), intra-regional tourism, intra-regional investment in the tourism sector, and, the development of a regional definition of tourism and of a regional policy towards cruise tourism.

The full implementation of regional integration under the CSME initiative provides opportunities for the transfer of goods, skills, and capital through the free movement of persons. It will allow CARICOM nationals with tourism and hospitality training and experience to take advantage of employment opportunities in the wider region. It will also enhance the flexibility and opportunities for CARICOM nationals to trade, invest, and establish tourism enterprises across borders.

Tourism is also a catalyst for intra-regional travel. The intra-regional component of tourism is not a substitute for tourists coming from outside of the region. It is, however, a value-added component to diversify the region's tourism product and spread the benefit of tourism development across the region. Intra-regional tourism provides vast economic exchange and opportunities for the regional economy that would have otherwise gone to countries such as the US, Canada, and England. This form of inward-looking tourism is also a practical approach to reversing the over-dependence of the region's tourism sector on international markets. Currently, the Caribbean Tourism Organization's (CTO) aviation task force is working with intra-Caribbean carriers to ensure hassle-free movement and to boost connectivity around the region. These include legal and regulatory concerns, safety and security issues, taxation and the high cost of airline tickets and the passenger's experience, which involves persons requiring a visa to travel.

One of the region's most noted successes in the area of promoting intra-regional tourism was the signing of the Multilateral Air Services Agreement (MASA) by CARICOM heads of government in March 2019. This landmark instrument is aimed at improving the level, quality, and efficiency of air services within and beyond the Caribbean Community through creating a liberalized environment consistent with emerging World Trade Organization (WTO) aviation policies. It is anticipated that the full implementation of MASA will improve connectivity and facilitate increased trade in goods and services, including tourism. MASA has been expanded to include the conditions for a single security check for direct transit passengers on multi-stop intra-Community flights.

Another component of deepening regional integration through tourism is the possibility of developing a regional tourism rating or classification scheme which could help improve quality and enhance the visitor experience, if sufficient resources could be devoted to agreeing on common standards and criteria and to managing the scheme impartially and effectively. Such scheme could ensure a level of quality assurance for visitors and stimulate product and service quality improvement through the objective benchmarking of visitor facilities and service standards. Synergy can also be achieved at the regional level by developing common training and certification standards and, where appropriate and affordable, delivering training programmes in a regional centre or online. Areas that could usefully be added to present hospitality and tourism curriculum and activities include management training, customer-handling skills such as foreign languages, events and attractions (including sports) management, and crisis recovery/disaster management.

Another way that tourism is being increasingly linked to regional economic integration is through the concept of a multidestination arrangement. There has been an emergent perspective that the future fortunes of the region may lie in economic convergence between complementary economies rather than in trying to make existing models of economic integration involving every CARICOM nation work. The suggestion was that economies of a similar size and level of development were complementary and could integrate better from an economic and commercial perspective. One consequence was that participants from the northern Caribbean, and in particular from Jamaica and the Dominican Republic, argued that there may be greater future value in Jamaica, Cuba, and the Dominican Republic being in a closer economic relationship that might also involve Cayman as a financial hub. The suggestion was that there were better opportunities for growth through a more rational approach to economic integration between geographically proximate, complementary economies linked to much improved transport infrastructure. This was not meant to replace CARICOM but to be a new route to economic convergence in the Caribbean basin. As a start, it was proposed that the countries and the industry could begin to work out practically how multidestination tourism might work between the four countries.

Considering this recommendation, Jamaica, along with Cuba, the Dominican Republic, and Mexico have entered into an agreement to roll out a multidestination offering to the international market for the 2018 winter tourist season. This new architecture revolves around the idea of enabling visitors to seamlessly travel to two, three, or more geographically proximate nations and stay over in each destination. We anticipate that this symbiotic arrangement will expand economic benefits of the tourism sector to approximately thirty-three million people. Overall, the tourism sector has vast untapped potential to promote the sustainable development of the region in ways that cuts across geographical boundaries. We must, thus, find common ground on a number of issues and strengthen our cooperation in a number of shared areas to ensure that tourism development truly brings us together.

6.2. Political Leadership and Tourism

As a minister of tourism for one of the world's most tourism-dependent countries in the world's most tourism-dependent region, I am in a safe position to say that the recent pandemic presented the greatest challenge to the sector that I have ever witnessed. As a consequence of the various containment measures that were introduced and sustained across countries, all of which would have curtailed public assembly as well as domestic and international travel, the tourism sector had to deal with a historic crisis that it was unable to respond to with any degree of confidence and certainty. Suddenly, all our previous gains as well as strategies that had seemingly worked well, up to two years prior, appeared inadequate to respond to the new demands of the pandemic era.

However, political leadership emerged as a distinct catalyst of the resilience and agility of countries during this crisis period. It became a crucial force for engendering national solidarity, harnessing the collective efforts of societies, mobilizing resources for social interventions and national responses, coordinating with both domestic and external stakeholders for positive outcomes and maintaining the balance between warning, activism, and assurance. Undoubtedly, given the unprecedented and prolonged disruption induced by the pandemic, effective leadership enabled Jamaica's tourism industry to remain buoyant and resilient. In the context of Jamaica, due to a combination of swift action, proactive leadership, effective communication and innovative thinking, we were able to quickly adapt and implement new health and safety protocols that guided the tourism sector's management of the pandemic in accordance with globally accepted standards. From the first positive case of COVID-19 was confirmed in April 2020, we began to actively engage all stakeholders: travel agencies, cruise lines, hoteliers, booking agencies, marketing agencies, airlines, WHTA, WTO, CTO, CHTA, etc. This was critical in ensuring that we continued to gain the confidence of the international community that the country was taking all the steps necessary to remain a safe and secure destination for all visitors. We also adopted a whole of society approach to the implementation and monitoring of protocols. For example, our five-point plan for the recovery of the tourism sector which emphasized the development of robust health and safety protocols, increased training for all segments of the tourism sector, building safety and security infrastructure, and acquiring PPE and hygiene tools was designed and implemented based on a public-private sector partnership consisting of key stakeholders including hoteliers, the Ministry of Tourism, the Ministry of Health, and various other agencies. Our eighty-eight-page COVID-19 mitigation protocols, developed for the whole sector, also received the endorsement of the World Travel and Tourism Council (WTTC) and complemented our highly successful Resilient Corridors to the north and south of the island, designed to keep workers, communities, and visitors safe by only opening areas/zones that we have the capacity to effectively monitor and manage. Beyond a commitment of safe reopening and quick recovery, the tourism sector's response to the pandemic paid attention to the human side.

Throughout 2020, the various agencies continued to provide critical support to small and medium tourism enterprises (SMTEs) within the industry that would have been reeling from the effects of COVID-19, including artisans and craft vendors, transportation providers, restaurants and eateries, bed and breakfasts, and farmers. A robust support structure was built out to support enterprises within the sector. The Tourism Enhancement Fund (TEF) collaborated with key partners to create several initiatives geared towards helping SMTEs retool and rebound from COVID-19, including the provision of resilience packages, loan facilitation, and grants provided through the Ministry of Finance and the Public Service. Throughout 2020, the Ministry of Tourism renewed its commitment to building human capital in the tourism industry to ensure a competitive and productive workforce that could meet the growing demand for specialized skills in the travel and tourism industry.

The ministry continued to provide certification to hundreds of tourism workers through partnerships between the Human Employment and Resource Training/National Service Training Agency Trust (HEART/NSTA Trust), Universal Service Fund (USF), National Restaurants Association (NRA), the American Hotel & Lodging Educational Institute (AHLEI), and Jamaica Centre of Tourism Innovation (JCTI), which is a division of the TEF, tasked specifically with facilitating the development of Jamaica's valuable human capital and supporting innovation for the tourism sector. The JCTI is currently offering middle management certification in areas such as Certified Food and Beverage Executive (CFBE); Certified Hospitality Housekeeping Executive (CHHE); Certified Hospitality Trainer (CHT), and Certified Hotel Concierge (CHC). Additionally, the recently introduced Hospitality and Tourism Management Programme (HTMP), administered in partnership with the Ministry of Education, Youth and Information, has produced graduates who are now in possession of entry-level tourism qualifications.

The ministry and its agencies also thought about the then new, health and safety requirements that would have shaped perceptions of destination security and attractiveness during this crisis period. Coinciding with the travel requirements for international travellers, we launched JAMAICA CARES to amplify the themes of safe and seamless travel. Jamaica Cares is an innovative end-to-end travel protection and emergency services programme that provides visitors with cost of medical care, evacuations, field rescue, case management, and patient advocacy caused by several factors, including natural disasters. As it relates to COVID-19, the protection plan also covered testing for symptomatic travellers, quarantine/isolation in a medical facility or sanctioned quarantine facilities and evacuation, if necessary. Overall, JAMAICA CARES galvanized a destination-wide COVID-19 response and encompassed our industry-leading Resilient Corridors, extensive health and safety protocols, entry testing, COVID-19 training for hospitality workers, travel authorization, and much more.

As we look to the future, the recent pandemic undoubtedly highlighted several critical considerations that must inform the future of the tourism sector. Recovery has become almost synonymous with resilience-building. The sector needs to be more adaptable, resilient, and agile. The pandemic presented a unique opportunity to transition towards a more balanced tourism as it is anticipated that more international tourists will opt for 'sustainable' destinations in this post-COVID era. Importantly, the sector must find ways to answer the question of how increasingly scarce natural resources can be prudently managed and how economic growth can be aligned with the social and economic needs of local populations and communities, as well as the preservation of the natural environment. Tourism-development strategies and practices must be increasingly designed to promote more resource efficient initiatives that are aligned with goals of sustainable consumption and production. Understanding the volatile and difficult environment within which they operate, we have come to terms with the fact that reducing the number of raw materials, energy, production, operating and disposal costs will increase the sector's bottom line.

Overall, the ministry and its agencies remain committed to nurturing a tourism sector that generates benefits for all involved in the value chain. We are cognizant that tourism is a resilient sector that has also bounced back from adversities. The strategic framework for resetting Jamaica's tourism has been guided by the Blue Ocean Strategy that will allow us to meet our growth targets of five million visitors, five billion dollars, and five thousand new rooms by 2025 in a sustainable manner. A Blue Ocean Strategy is the simultaneous pursuit of differentiation and low cost to open up a new market space and create new demand. It is about creating and capturing uncontested market space, thereby making the competition irrelevant. It is based on the view that market boundaries and industry structure are not a given and can be reconstructed by the actions and beliefs of industry players. A Blue Ocean Strategy calls for the creation of business models that depart from traditional models based on competition and standardization. It will see our ministry pursuing enhanced value-creation, through product differentiation and diversification, which will allow Destination Jamaica to appeal to new markets and stimulate new demands. Over the long term, a vital component of the Blue Ocean Strategy will be to strengthen the systems for tourism zoning and theming so that the unique characteristics of each destination area will be preserved and enhanced to support their own distinct brand appeal.

Resetting Jamaica's tourism also requires the identification and establishment of innovative policies, systems, protocols, and standards that will assure our visitors a safer, secure, and seamless experience while building out a new national tourism model based on a diversified portfolio of unique and authentic attractions and activities, which draw heavily on Jamaica's natural and cultural assets and ensure that more locals can participate in and benefit from the tourism sector.

I am also fully aware that the country's vision for sustainable development will only be realized if our governance framework emphasizes and promotes key values, such as transparency and accountability, meritocracy, integrity and honesty, genuine consultation and cooperation, inclusiveness and responsiveness, mutual respect, and a focus on long-term national goals rather than short term political imperatives. I fully understand and accept my responsibility to ensure that a framework of good governance is firmly established and maintained to promote sustainable development. Otherwise, people will lose trust in the institutions of the state and disengage themselves from society. The essence of good governance is described as predictable, open, and enlightened policy, together with a bureaucracy imbued with a professional ethos and an executive arm of government accountable for its actions. The mandate of VISION 2030 to make 'Jamaica the place of choice to live, work, raise families and do business' will be no more than a pipedream if citizens lack confidence in the capacity of state institutions and organs to be fair, corrupt-free, and transparent and to effect social, economic, and political transformation. This understanding was the basis for the announcement that all members of the Cabinet will be exposed to good governance training as a measure to safeguard against corruption, as the government seeks to restore the public's confidence in the integrity of our institutions of government. However, the solutions to the country's problems do not rest with government alone. The sum total of our potential exceeds our problems; our collective capabilities are greater than our challenge. Indeed, governance includes the state but transcends it by considering the private sector and civil society, all of which are critical in promoting and sustaining development. The government is therefore committed to a model of partnership which will allow us to utilize all our strengths and capabilities for greater impact, as we position Jamaica as the place of choice to live, work, raise families, and do business. Sustainable development can only be realized by deepening the partnership process and the ownership by the wider society of national development plans and goals, through ongoing dialogue and agreed actions based on mutual respect and a commitment to genuine cooperation, meaningful consultation, and honest communication.

The institutions of governance in the state, civil society, and the private sector must be designed to contribute to this sustainable development by establishing the political, legal, economic, and social circumstances for poverty reduction, job creation, environmental protection, and the advancement of women. We continue to strengthen partnerships with those who share similar values, principles, goals, and aspirations for peace and security, good governance and the rule of law, for the ultimate objective of securing development and prosperity for all our people. Jamaica currently has in place a coalition framework for promoting participatory governance known as the Partnership for a Prosperous Jamaica (PFPJ), which includes the state, represented by the government and the Opposition, the private sector, the trade unions and civil society ('the Partners'). The Partners have all accepted their responsibility to deepening democracy and participatory decision-making, to encourage meaningful participation of all Partners in national development, to build trust and confidence among the Partners, and to develop a framework with supporting institutions for conducting ongoing relations, negotiations, and transformative actions among the Partners.

From a sustainable development standpoint, the Partners recognize that the severity of the country's social and economic problems require a national call to action and as such they have committed to initiating and supporting national efforts to accelerate the growth of the economy, improving justice and security, enhancing gender equality, empowering young people, protecting the environment, enhancing enterprise competitiveness in pursuit of growth and development with equity, improving education, research, and health outcomes, promoting accountability and transparency, and harnessing the positive contributions and resources of the dynamic diaspora.

The state has sought to ensure that the country's key development priorities are aligned with the imperatives of the globally acknowledged sustainable development goals (SGDs) in the areas of sustained economic growth and development, equity, security and safety, good health, world-class education and training, good governance, innovation, environmental sustainability, and climate change adaptation. The SDGs and Vision 2030 Jamaica – National Development Plan fully and adequately provide us with the framework for achieving sustainable development through the integration of economic, social, and environmental dimensions.

Overall, innovation is now perhaps the most important catalyst for promoting good governance and sustainable development in

Jamaica. The effective use of innovation will help to modernize the country's public sector, enhance the government's responsiveness to citizens and firms' demand for more flexible and seamless access to government services, reduce bureaucracy and proceduralism, facilitate the broader participation of society in governance, increase state capacity to connect with and better serve marginalized groups, and to better implement, monitor, and evaluate policy outcomes.

6.3. Global Inclusive Growth and Tourism

Tourism remains the engine of economic growth, job creation, and development in many countries around the world. It is especially crucial to the livelihoods of undiversified island economies. The value chain of the tourism industry quite often extends beyond opportunities for direct employment and earnings for tourism enterprises. It also incorporates several other segments of national economies with which the sector maintains vital economic linkages including manufacturing, agriculture, services, and the cultural and creative industries. For the foreseeable future, tourism will continue to be a fundamental pillar of the world economy. Notwithstanding, the disruptive forces of COVID-19 have thrusted important conversations about the viability of current models of tourism development to meet future challenges. In particular, it is easily recognizable that the tourism product in most parts of the developing world is heavily tied to the natural environment. The UNWTO, for example, notes that maritime or ocean-related tourism, as well as coastal tourism are vital sectors of the economy in small island developing States (SIDS) and coastal least developed countries (LDCs). Thus, tourism development in many contexts might be likened to a double-edged sword as the growth, development, and expansion of the tourism product quite often threaten environmental sustainability. Admittedly, among other resources, the hospitality industry uses substantial amounts of energy for providing comfort and services to its guests, typically with a low level of energy efficiency.

Energy supply, vital for the tourism industry, is still dominated by oil products which increase islands' vulnerability to the environmental impact of fossil-fuel use, as well as to oil price volatility, which makes it difficult for the industry to remain competitive. Currently, the global tourism industry is responsible for 5–8 per cent of all global greenhouse gas (GHG) emissions, including flights, maritime and land transport, hotel construction and operation, and air conditioning and heating. Overall, tourism is both a victim of, and contributor to climate change. While tourism activities help to contribute to environmental phenomena, such as rising sea levels, melting glaciers, floods, avalanches, water scarcity, deforestation, biodiversity loss, desertification, wildfires, drought and diseases, at the same time, these phenomena also hurt the tourism economy.

In recent years, development policy discourses have begun to scrutinize traditional model of tourism because of its negative impacts on the environment, local communities, and cultural heritage, as well as the widespread view that the benefits of tourism are very often concentrated and do not sufficiently trickle down to local populations and communities. As concerns about sustainability and social inclusion have gained traction, the concept of sustainable tourism has emerged as a way to balance the economic, social, and environmental aspects of tourism. The Rio+20 outcome document entitled 'The Future We Want' described sustainable tourism as a significant contributor to the three dimensions of sustainable development – the environment, the economy, and society – because of its close linkages to other sectors and its ability to create decent jobs and generate trade opportunities. It consequently urged member states to recognize:

> *the need to support sustainable tourism activities and relevant capacity building that promote environmental awareness, conserve and protect the environment, respect wildlife, flora, biodiversity, ecosystems and cultural diversity, and improve the welfare and livelihoods of local communities by supporting their local economies and the human and natural environment as a whole.*

Closely related to the concept of sustainable tourism is tourism resilience which refers to 'the ability of a destination or tourism system to cope with, adapt to, and recover from shocks and disruptions, such as natural disasters, pandemics, economic crises, and climate change impacts.' As the frequency of disruptive events such as hurricanes, wildfires, disease outbreaks, and geopolitical tensions increases and further magnifies the vulnerability of tourism destinations and businesses to various risks, the concept of tourism resilience has increasingly occupied an important place in the global discourse on sustainable tourism, emphasizing the need to build the capacity for resilience in tourism destinations and communities to ensure their long-term viability and competitiveness. A key aspect of tourism resilience is *socio-economic resilience*, which entails maximizing the tourism sector's ability to promote social inclusion, economic diversification, and community engagement in tourism development. Sustainable tourism should contribute to poverty reduction, social cohesion, and local community well-being and reduce inequality and marginalization. Strategies for enhancing socio-economic resilience in tourism destinations include promoting local ownership and control of tourism resources, facilitating community-based tourism initiatives, providing training and capacity building opportunities for local communities, and fostering cultural preservation and heritage conservation

Another key aspect of tourism resilience is *environmental resilience*. This thrust recognizes that tourism and environmental resilience are intertwined as the sustainability of tourism destinations depends heavily on the health and preservation of natural resources and ecosystems. Thus, for its own long-term viability, the tourism sector needs to make environmental resilience a core focus and prioritize safeguarding the natural environment and mitigating the negative impacts of tourism on ecosystems and biodiversity. Climate change, in particular, is an environmental phenomenon that has significant implications for the tourism sector. The impacts of climate change on tourism are multifaceted and complex, ranging from direct impacts on natural resources and attractions, to indirect impacts on transportation, accommodation, and tourist behaviour. Climate change can also exacerbate existing vulnerabilities in tourism destinations, such as those related to poverty, inequality, and inadequate infrastructure.

One of the most significant direct impacts of climate change on tourism is the loss or degradation of natural resources and attractions that are germane for tourism activities, such as beaches, coral reefs, forests, and wildlife habitats. For example, rising sea levels and more frequent and severe storms can result in beach erosion, coastal flooding, and damage to coastal infrastructure, which can negatively impact coastal tourism destinations. Similarly, coral bleaching due to warmer ocean temperatures can reduce the attractiveness of coral reef destinations for snorkelling and diving, which can have adverse effects on local economies that rely on marine tourism. Against the backdrop provided, collective action is urgently required to maximize the tourism sector's capacity to promote sustainable and inclusive growth. At the culmination of the United Nations Climate Change Conference (COP26) held in Glasgow in 2021, tourism was recognized as an established part of the UN agenda, recognized for its ability to contribute to all the sustainable development goals. The UNWTO then gave its commitment to the bridging of the gap between governments and the private sector to ensure tourism lives up to its climate action responsibilities. Specifically, the Glasgow Declaration with over 150 signatories from every part of the sector and every size, reflected the sector's firm commitment to accelerating the sector's shift to net-zero. At the same time, however, it was also acknowledged that the efforts of industry stakeholders need to be backed by broader support if the desired goals are to be achieved. This point underscores the need for coordination, strong actions, political and financial support for tourism's transition to greater inclusivity and sustainability.

Collaboration and coordination should reflect a whole of society approach that incorporates internal and external stakeholders, including governments, businesses, local communities, NGOs, think tanks, academia, and travellers. The end goal of this collaborative approach is to ensure that the tourism sector plays a critical role in mitigating climate change by adopting sustainable practices, investing in green infrastructure, promoting responsible tourism behaviours, and raising awareness among travellers. More specifically, meaningful collaboration and partnerships are required to develop climate-resilient infrastructure, promote nature-based solutions, and integrate climate risk assessments into tourism planning and management. There is an urgent need for increased funding and investment to enable sustainable tourism practices and infrastructure. This includes investments in renewable energy, green transportation, eco-friendly accommodation, and waste management systems that reduce carbon emissions, minimize environmental impacts, and promote sustainable resource use.

There is a need also for greater research and innovation to develop new technologies, solutions, and best practices that can help the tourism industry adapt to climate change and reduce its carbon footprint. This includes advancements in renewable energy, water conservation, waste management, and sustainable transportation options, such as electric vehicles and public transportation systems.

Finally, there is also a need for increased awareness and education among travellers about the impacts of climate change on tourism and the importance of sustainable travel choices. Travellers should be encouraged to choose destinations, accommodations, and activities that are environmentally responsible and support local communities. This can be achieved through educational campaigns, certifications, and labelling schemes that promote sustainable tourism practices. Ultimately, sustainable tourism practices, infrastructure, and policies are essential for mitigating the impacts of climate change on tourism destinations, protecting natural resources, preserving cultural heritage, and ensuring the long-term sustainability of the tourism industry. It is therefore imperative that all stakeholders in the tourism industry come together to take concerted action to combat climate change and secure a sustainable future for tourism.

7. Promoting Sustainability in Tourism

7.1. Sustainable Tourism

The Ministry of Tourism continues to place high value on the input of its network of partners which include hoteliers, the business community, arts and craft vendors, farmers, service providers, and community-based enterprises. Indeed, our Tourism Linkages Council currently comprises of public and private sector partners who oversee the coordination and implementation of effective and sustainable strategies. We strongly believe that the appropriate tourism governance framework for sustainable development will require a whole of society approach promoting the tenets of mutual respect, consensus-building, and participatory decision-making.

As the minister of tourism of an island nation that is facing, head on, several simultaneous threats to its sustainable development, including climate change and global warning, depleting natural resources, beach erosion, biodiversity loss, frequent natural disasters, high energy consumption, and vulnerability to epidemics and pandemics, I am always eager to discuss the exigency of promoting sustainable strategies for tourism development.

The recent pandemic undoubtedly magnified many of the sustainable challenges facing the tourism product in small island developing states. This has necessitated a firm commitment among policymakers, industry leaders, and other tourism stakeholders to support a change in policies, business practices, and consumer behaviour towards a more sustainable tourism sector that can contribute to the attainment of the Universal 2030 Agenda for Sustainable Development and the Sustainable Development Goals (SDGs), particularly in areas such as promoting inclusive and sustainable economic growth, social inclusiveness, employment and poverty reduction, resource efficiency, environmental protection and climate change, cultural values, diversity and heritage and mutual understanding, peace and security. As previously mentioned, the pandemic presented a unique opportunity to transition towards a more balanced tourism as it is anticipated that more international tourists will opt for 'sustainable' destinations in the post-COVID era. Overall, we now have a watershed moment to align the effort of sustaining livelihoods dependent on tourism to the SDGs and ensuring a more resilient, inclusive, carbon neutral, and resource- efficient future.

Current models of tourism built around laissez-faire behaviours and that emphasize quantity over quality must give way to new enlightened approaches emphasizing sustainability. Tourism and environmental sustainability do not have to be opposed to each other. They can, in fact, be complementary but requires that that the sector shifts to sustainable energy collected from renewable sources, meaning those which are naturally replenished, such as solar from sunlight, wind, water from rain, tides, waves, and geothermal heat, natural resources to which many tourism establishments have access. Examples of renewable energy include solar panels, solar water heaters, wind turbines, bio-digestors, fully solar-powered refrigerators/freezers, solar lights, and hydro systems. Other notable innovations in the area of renewable energy include solar air conditioning (SAC), seawater air conditioning (SWAC), and solar photovoltaic (PV) systems. Among the benefits of the shift to renewable energy are cost savings, better competitiveness due to reduced cost, reduction of carbon footprint, environmentally friendly image for businesses allowing for new markets, an improvement on the quality of services offered to guests, and preparation for future problems, such as power outages and water shortages. Beyond the use of renewable energy sources, the adoption of energy conservation and eco-friendly practices will be required at every stage of the building and management process. This includes selecting an appropriate building site, using sustainable building materials, implementing green energy sources, and applying a natural design style.

Indeed, the sustainability of coastal tourism destinations depends partly on their ability to adapt planning and management practices to the impacts of climate change and also to increase their ability to effectively manage natural disaster. Climate change mitigation strategies will involve technological, economic, and social changes, use of alternatives and changed behaviours among tourists, with objectives to reduce greenhouse gas emissions. In terms of operational efficiency and energy cost reductions, more tourism businesses must embrace Energy-saving technologies, such as sensors, LED, smart climate control, embrace recycling, water harvesting, reduce plastic use and increase reusable goods, such as reusable napkins, glasses, straws, water bottles, cups, linen, etc.

Realizing the key sustainability goals requires that tourism stakeholders address gaps and deficiencies within current operational frameworks. Stakeholders must become more proactive, vigilant, and must constantly evaluate their capacities to counter old and emergent challenges. This includes forming standards for vulnerability assessments and risk mapping, strengthening collaborations, embracing innovations, enhancing information-sharing, and coordinating policy design across multiple internal and external stakeholders.

7.2. The Role of the Insurance Industry in Promoting Sustainability

In all its history, the international economy and marketplace has never been more volatile and unpredictable. Businesses across all sectors and industries are simultaneously exposed to wide-ranging risks, including property damage, data breaches, work-related accidents and casualties, vehicular damage, product liability, errors and omissions, business hazards, natural hazards, business interruption among others. Given the unpredictable nature of these risks coupled with the limited financial bases of many businesses, especially SMEs, risk transfer through enrolment in insurance schemes has become a very crucial factor of successful business management in the modern context. This is against the backdrop that the majority of SMEs, especially in the tourism sector, do not survive beyond a decade after being established while for others, survival is a constant struggle with factors, such as the inability to properly manage risks being singled out as a crucial factor.

Overall, in the post-COVID era, the insurance industry will become a key component of risk management and disaster financing mechanisms, especially in the cases of global threats that have wide-ranging impacts on the structure and functioning of the global economy and financial system. Thus, underinsured businesses or businesses operating without broad and adequate levels of insurance coverage are exposing themselves to great financial risks that can lead to acute business interruptions, business collapse, and bankruptcy. The tourism industry is no stranger to disruptive events. While it is generally considered one of the most resilient segments of the global economy, exhibiting the propensity to rebound quickly from shocks, the tourism sector remains extremely vulnerable to disruptive events linked to phenomena, such as natural disasters, global warming and climate change, environmental degradation, epidemics and pandemics, terror attacks, economic recessions, and cyber insecurity. The recent COVID-19 pandemic has highlighted the significant threat that unforeseen and prolonged disasters and disruptions can present for the tourism value chain in Jamaica, which incorporates other segments of the national economy with which tourism has traditionally established vital linkages, such as agriculture, manufacturing, gastronomy, transportation, export trade, foreign exchange, entertainment, and the craft industry. As the tourism sector continues to rebound and prepare for future shocks, the insurance industry has a critical role in supporting organizations, as they start their sustainability journeys, by identifying and helping them navigate and manage new and emerging physical, transition and liability risks, such as supply-chain interruptions, risks related to climate change and global warming, new technologies, and delays to projects.

The role of the insurance industry in promoting sustainable tourism growth has already been formally recognized. For example, the United Nations Framework Convention on Climate Change (UNFCCC) in Article 4.8 calls for actions related to funding, insurance, and the transfer of technology, to meet the specific needs and concerns of developing country arising from the adverse effects of climate change and/or the impact of the implementation of response measures. More recently, the World Travel and Tourism Council (WTTC), in unveiling its insurance guidelines to rebuild global consumer confidence to help encourage the return of travelling, described the insurance industry as 'a vital part of the travel and tourism experience, providing peace of mind and risk mitigation to consumers, suppliers, and organizations across the travel and tourism sector.' From the perspective of sustainability in the tourism sector, the most urgent challenge confronting tourism enterprises is climate change adaptation. The insurance industry is being called upon to accelerate its investment in global climate modelling and exploring ways to drive the necessary changes. In this regard, key shifts that should drive the new thinking of the insurance industry towards climate resilience for susceptible sectors such as tourism include encouraging risk management practices, incentivizing environmentally friendly behaviours, and driving investments towards sustainable initiatives. Just as the insurance industry has historically minimized risks from building fires, earthquakes, and improved auto safety, it has a huge opportunity to develop creative solutions and products that will reduce climate-change-related losses for consumers, the government and insurers.

The role of the insurance industry in promoting the sustainable transition of the tourism industry is multifold. Insurance companies assess and facilitate the transfer of risks associated with various aspects of the tourism sector, such as natural disasters, climate change impacts, and health crises. By offering coverage against these risks, insurance companies encourage businesses to adopt measures that reduce vulnerability to environmental hazards. This includes promoting sustainable construction practices, reducing carbon footprint, and encouraging the use of renewable energy. Insurance companies can also help businesses to design sustainable investment strategies. As insurance companies manage significant investment portfolios, they have the potential to influence sustainable development in the tourism industry by considering environmental, social, and governance (ESG) factors in their investment decisions. By directing their investments toward sustainable tourism projects, such as eco-friendly accommodations and renewable-energy initiatives, insurers can support the growth of responsible tourism practices.

The insurance industry can also support product innovation. This entails the development of specialized products that cater to the unique risks and challenges faced by the tourism sector in promoting sustainability. For example, they can offer coverage for ecotourism activities, carbon offsetting programmes, smart technology adoption, green or renewable energy transition, and liability protection for sustainable tourism operators. To incentivize the adoption of sustainable tourism products, insurance companies can offer premium reductions or discounts to tourism businesses that implement environmentally friendly practices. This may encourage more tourism enterprise to adopt eco-friendly measures and reduce their environmental impact.

The impact of the insurance industry in promoting sustainable transition in the tourism sector will also involve its pivotal role in knowledge-sharing. This entails collaborations between insurance companies and other stakeholders, such as tourism associations, government agencies, and environmental organizations, to share knowledge and best practices for promoting sustainability. They can provide insights on risk management, sustainable investment strategies, and emerging trends to support the development of sustainable tourism policies and initiatives.

Equally, insurance companies can support capacity-building through the provision of training and education programmes for tourism businesses that focus on risk management, resilience planning, and sustainable practices, helping businesses understand the importance of sustainability and equipping them with the necessary tools to implement responsible measures. Finally, insurance companies can promote advocacy and awareness by leveraging their influence to advocate for sustainable policies and practices within the tourism industry. By raising awareness about the risks of unsustainable tourism and promoting the benefits of responsible practices, insurance companies can encourage tourism businesses, policymakers, and travellers to prioritize sustainability.

Two dimensions or types of risk transfer that will increasingly define the role of the insurance in promoting sustainability in the post-COVID-19 period are parametric insurance and travel insurance. The exposure of industries, such as tourism to natural disasters, makes parametric insurance, also known as event-based insurance or index-based insurance, a more attractive disaster financing mechanism for players in the tourism sector when compared to traditional disaster risk indemnity insurance schemes. This is because parametric insurance insures a policyholder against the occurrence of a specific event by paying a set amount based on the magnitude of the event, as opposed to the magnitude of the losses in a traditional indemnity policy. In other words, in the event of the occurrence of a natural disaster, there would be no need to measure or verify damages or for the policyholder to initiate a claim; the parametric insurance is automatically triggered when the objective event happens. This type of contract allows disbursements to reach policyholders much faster with payments disbursed in matter of weeks with a parametric contract, versus months or years with a standard indemnity contract. Firms, insuring against business interruption risk, government agencies responsible for disaster response, and non-governmental organizations (NGOs) providing assistance all benefit from receiving pay-out faster because resources can be deployed more rapidly at the most critical time, right after the disaster has struck. This is crucial to enhancing response time, ensuring minimal disruption, as well as speedy recovery, which are all crucial factors of sustainability.

Equally, travel insurance is emerging as an important element of enhancing destination attractiveness and security, especially in the aftermath of COVID-19, an event which has helped to magnify the importance of enhancing healthy and safety standards for travellers. Tourist destinations globally are being increasingly called upon to adopt the directive of the Global Code of Ethics for Tourism, adopted by the UNWTO General Assembly in October 1999, which stated that tourism professionals, should work with public authorities to take care of the safety of tourists, such as accident prevention, health and food hygiene for those who request their services, and that they must ensure that adequate insurance and assistance systems are in place. Data reveal that the global travel insurance market grew from $19.14 billion in 2022 to $22.44 billion in 2023 at a compound annual growth rate (CAGR) of 17.3 per cent and is expected to grow to $40.58 billion in 2027 at a CAGR of 16.0 per cent. The most beneficial covers on a travel insurance policy are coverage for trip cancellations, medical emergencies, travel delays, and luggage protection. Overall, travel insurance provides an added layer of security and peace of mind for international travellers who will increasingly opt for destinations offering such coverage. I am proud to say that Jamaica is a regional leader in this innovation, having recently introduced 'Jamaica Cares' which is a groundbreaking travel insurance programme that provides all visitors to Jamaica with access to traveller protection and medical services and guarantees a first-of-its-kind suite of medical emergency management and travel insurance from departure to return.

In total, the insurance industry plays a vital role in promoting sustainability by driving positive changes in the business landscape and society as a whole. Through their risk assessment and mitigation practices, insurers encourage businesses to adopt sustainable practices and technologies, reducing their environmental impact and promoting long-term resilience. Overall, the insurance industry's commitment to sustainability extends beyond its core business of risk management. By integrating sustainable practices into their operations, promoting green initiatives, and investing in a sustainable future, insurers are making significant contributions to environmental protection, social well-being, and economic stability. Their efforts are crucial in addressing the challenges of climate change and fostering a more sustainable and resilient world for future generations.

7.3. Tourism from Anthropause to Anthropulse

After more than two years of tireless efforts to balance economic survival with the protection of the health and wellness of global populations, through a range of restrictive measures, it is certainly welcomed news that the last several months have been favourable to the imminent downgrading of COVID-19 from a pandemic to epidemic. This is based on the evidence that global infection rates have declined precipitously with the World Health Organization indicating that COVID-19 cases are down at least 17 per cent globally. As more and more countries record reduced rates of COVID-19 infection and transmission, they have incrementally eased many restrictions for citizens who are fully vaccinated such as mask mandates, limit on public gatherings, social distancing, travel bans, mandatory quarantine, and stay-at-home and work-from-home orders. The relaxation of restrictions has laid the foundation for speedy recovery of the global economy and the eventual return of billions of citizens to many of the habits, cultures, lifestyles, and activities that they have enjoyed before the pandemic.

Despite the obvious importance of societies returning to some semblance of normalcy as soon as possible, this excitement was expected to be tempered by the recognition that the pandemic has produced unprecedented changes to the world in which we live that must be carefully considered so that we can forecast their impact for the future. One of the more far-reaching impacts of the pandemic has been described by many scholars as the 'great reset,' a term that suggests that the ecological, social, geopolitical, and economic impacts of the pandemic have taken societies back to a period that some have likened to the beginning of times. From the perspective of its ecological or environmental impact, a group of researchers coined the term 'Anthropause' to describe the period of unusual planetary calm caused by early COVID-19 lockdowns. The phenomenon allows us to make observations about the reaction of nature or the environment to the slowdown of human activity caused by the COVID-19 pandemic.

In recent history, the COVID-19 pandemic undoubtedly caused the most sustained global reductions in human mobility and physical interactions between human beings and the natural environment. When the pandemic was first declared in 2020, countries went into lockdown, borders were closed, streets, cities and towns were vacated, and many popular tourism destinations experienced little to no traffic. The experiences over the past two years ultimately provided scientists with the opportunity to examine how nature has responded to the resultant dramatic deceleration of the physical interaction of human beings with the natural environment and the various forms of pollution and degradation emanate from it. By using data collected with tiny animal-attached electronic devices called 'bio-loggers,' the team of scientists who coined the phenomenon, amassed more than one billion GPS location records for some thirteen thousand tagged animals from all around the world – including birds, mammals, and a variety of marine species, that allowed them to draw important conclusions. Their analysis confirmed positive outcomes such as fewer animals being killed by vehicles, return of some migrant and endangered species of animals. Other positive environmental benefits recorded elsewhere included improvement in global air quality due to lower anthropogenic emissions of air pollutants and atmospheric particles, recuperation of water ecosystems in some countries, restoration of some aquatic life due to reduced commercial fishing and less soil pollution due to significant reduction of solid and water waste. These observations seem to support the view that, as a consequence of the pandemic, nature appeared to have recovered or is 'taking over again.' Scientists have, however, cautioned that the return to normalcy is likely to endanger the sustainability gains realized as a result of the experience of 'anthropause.'

The belief among these scientists is that, as COVID-19 travel restrictions ease, a surge in human mobility and travel activity beyond pre-pandemic levels would appear imminent. They warn that this will lead to an outcome that they have described as 'Anthropulse' which will produce the opposite effect of anthropause by reversing recent environmental gains and dramatically accelerating environmental degradation. This is as people who are keen to make up for time lost over the last two years are likely to simultaneously intensify their return to a wide range of economic, social, and cultural activities will place added stress on the natural world. A new study conducted by Travel Pulse, for example, found that people planned more travel in 2022 due to being less concerned about the impact of the COVID-19 outbreak.

While the threat of anthropulse is well-founded, I strongly believe that the slowdown in human mobility witnessed between 2020 and 2022, presented opportunities for the tourism sector that can be maximized. Indeed, there was certainly an opportunity for Destination Jamaica to position itself to tap into the pent-up demand for international travel and to appeal to more diverse outbound tourism markets by aggressively marketing itself as a safe and secure destination option for visitors. However, to preserve the environmental benefits that have emerged since the pandemic's onset, we must intensify the pursuit of tourism strategies that cultivate an even stronger dedication to sustainable practices. This approach strives to achieve a harmonious balance between economic concerns and environmental well-being. The shift to sustainable tourism will not only allow Jamaica to compete for the growing number of international tourists who are expected to opt for more sustainable destinations in the post-pandemic era, but it will also allow Jamaica to accelerate the development of niche markets in sustainable tourism that the country is naturally suited for. These include ecotourism, health and wellness tourism, cultural and heritage tourism, and community tourism. While we diversify the tourism product with a view to promote sustainability, we must collaborate closely with all partners, especially hoteliers, to build capacities and commitment to the transitioning to alternative and renewable energy in the delivery of in-house tourism services. Ultimately, despite the general evidence to the contrary, I believe tourism and environmental development need not be in conflict with each other. As minister of tourism, I am committed to ensuring this.

8.
Cruise Tourism and Beyond

8.1. The Cruise Tourism

Globally, cruise tourism has been widely impacted by COVID-19 which forced border closures in major cruise tourism destinations in in North America, Europe, Asia-Pacific, and South America. In dramatic fashion, several cruise lines were met with no entry signs at various ports, resulting in stranding or forced return to port of exit. The cruise ship segment was especially vulnerable to the COVID-19 outbreak because of its tendency to attracting older passengers. One cruise line, in particular, the *Ruby Princess*, became the epicentre of the pandemic in Europe, with 340 cases at last count. So far, the calculated loss of the cruise tourism industry since the pandemic is at least US$750 million. Shares in major cruise companies such as Royal Caribbean, Carnival, and Norwegian have also dropped by 60–70 per cent.

In the Caribbean, most destinations had not received any cruise ship since February 2021 as major companies temporarily suspended sailings. The downturn in cruise tourism certainly had negative implications for Jamaica. Over the years, cruise tourism has rapidly evolved into one of the most crucial segments of the national economy, growing by over 300 per cent within the last ten years. Jamaica has been consistently ranked as the leading cruise destination in the region. The growth and development of the cruise industry segment has been buoyed by the country's substantial investments to upgrade ports to expand their carrying capacity. At the beginning of 2020, the projection was that cruise tourism would experience an uptick throughout 2020 with the entry of several new carriers such as Royal Caribbean's Symphony of the Seas. In January of this year, before the impact of COVID-19, Port Royal became the country's newest cruise port and welcomed its first ship call. Globally, cruise tourism was also the fastest growing sector of the global tourism industry before the pandemic. Evidently, the disruptive impact of the COVID-19 pandemic has derailed growth forecasts and recent growth trends in cruise tourism. Cruise tourism, has, however, traditionally been one of the most resilient segments of the global tourism industry.

Historically, the cruise tourism sector has been the most well-equipped and experienced in managing and monitoring health conditions of passengers and crew. As a part of their routine operational framework, cruise lines had implemented outbreak prevention and response measures and ships were fitted with medical facilities while shipboard and shore side medical professionals were available around the clock, 24/7, to provide initial medical care in the event of illness and prevent disease transmission. Cruise lines had also taken precautions to conduct passive as well as active screening of passengers and crew for illness prior to boarding when circumstances demanded. Due to these measures, the cruise industry was able to successfully manage infectious outbreaks in the past including H1N1, influenza, measles, legionnaires, and norovirus. Research has shown that cruise bookings in the past have returned to pre-event levels after about ninety days, which offers some optimism in the current situation. The global cruise tourism industry was also quick to respond to the recent pandemic. Its response has always prioritized the health and safety of passengers, crew, and the communities in the places visited. Following the WHO's declaration of a pandemic in mid-March 2020, all cruise lines registered with the Cruise Lines International Association (CLIA) made the unprecedented decision to voluntarily suspend worldwide operations, making the cruise industry one of the first to do so. This helped to minimize the direct threat of the COVID-19 to millions of cruise passengers and workers.

The CLIA also worked with local and national governments around the world, as well as leading health authorities and its partners across the wider cruise community to coordinate efforts during the ongoing suspension of worldwide cruise operations. Cruise lines also adopted pre-board screening and denying boarding to those who had recently travelled from or through affected areas consistent with prevailing guidance from global health authorities. The proactiveness of industry leaders certainly helped cruise tourism to fare significantly better than most other segments of the global tourism. The CLIA reported that the vast majority of more than 270 cruise ships within the CLIA member fleet were not affected by this virus. For our part, we have identified the recovery of the cruise tourism sector as a main priority. We activated the Tourism Recovery task Force, which was tasked with the general responsibility of developing a recovery and growth stimulation framework for the sector. Specific to cruise tourism, we also activated the 'Cruise Recovery Program', chaired by president and CEO of the Port Authority of Jamaica, Gordon Shirley. The minister of health also announced that a health protocol was being considered that would require airline and cruise-ship visitors to Jamaica to present medical certificates of a negative COVID-19 test before entering the island when the country reopens for international tourism. The medical certificate must not have been older than seventy-six hours. The Ministry of Tourism continued to actively monitor the crisis, communicate updates and identify collaborative strategies, with the goal of ensuring recovery of the sector in the shortest time possible.

8.2. Multidestination Arrangements, Opportunities, and Challenges

The growing interest in and demand for experiential tourism has forced destinations around the world to reconsider how they view the whole notion of competitiveness. One of the drivers of tourism competitiveness is the ability of destinations to develop more tourism products and packages that satisfy the growing need of international travellers for diverse, authentic, and gratifying experiences. As more destinations seek to promote experiential travel, one innovation that more destinations can consider to optimize visitors' experiences is the concept of 'multidestination arrangements.' This is a unique approach to tourism that enables a tourist to be able to visit and enjoy the offerings of multiple destinations during one trip at one cost. Currently, the only offering in international tourism that closely resembles a multi-destination arrangement is cruise shipping, whereby travellers aboard cruise ships are able to disembark at various ports within the cruise ship's sailing route. This, however, cannot be considered a multi-destination arrangement as the period of dismemberment is very brief, controlled, and does not allow travellers the freedom or opportunity to fully enjoy the full trappings of multiple destinations at their convenience.

A multi-destination arrangement is based on joint partnerships involving governments, airlines, hotels, tour operators, and attractions that will enable visitors to seamlessly travel to two, three, or more geographically proximate nations and stay over in each destination. Regions with shared or proximal borders, rich cultural and natural assets, and undiversified tourism products should have a greater incentive to explore multi-destination arrangements. This would give more destinations in such regions, especially the ones that are lesser known and developed, the opportunity to overcome inherent weaknesses, as it relates to marketing, exposure, and promotion while at the same time allowing them to profit more from their unique tourism offerings and products. It is indeed true that no single destination may be able to offer each tourist the full range of experiences that he or she craves. There are distinctions across destinations in terms of local languages, customs, cultures, architecture, biodiversity, cuisine, attractions, and sites. A genuine multi-destination arrangement will enable tourists to have multiple unique experiences that satisfy their travel interests in one trip.

Multi-destination arrangements are aligned with the broader push to align the tourist sector with regional integration and development. Regionalism has been long established as a viable framework for promoting integration and cooperation in trade and other areas to enhance a region's competitiveness, deepen its integration into the global economy, and address major socio-economic problems, such as poverty and unemployment. Generally, tourism tends to favour the circulation of people, capital, goods, and knowledge, which can positively impact economic and cultural integration. Overall, the tourism industry is highly competitive and demands sustainable and innovative marketing strategies to ensure long-term success. This has made it increasingly necessary to strengthen co-operation networks between countries, so as to increase and better share the revenues generated by tourism.

Exploring multi-destination arrangements reflects a response to the call made by the UNWTO for various regional governments to explore incentives and strategies to strengthen regional carriers; enhance intra-regional travel; and through joint airlift agreements, increase linkages between regional and international airlines as part of a broad-based strategy to boost tourist arrivals. The promotion of multi-destination arrangements in tourism is consistent with the growing view by tourism experts that the future fortunes of the tourism industry in specific regions region may lie in economic convergence between complementary economies rather stand-alone approaches. The suggestion is that economies of a similar size with shared vulnerabilities, similar level of development and shared geographical borders integrate better from an economic and commercial perspective. This would constitute a rational approach to economic integration that will allow the benefits of tourism to be spread across more economies in a region, thereby generating more economic opportunities for a greater number of people.

To overcome challenges and limitations of some destinations within a region, it has been suggested that a region can gain a competitive advantage and thus enhance sustainability if it can package and market its varied attractions more cohesively to entice potential visitors. Thus, the value of a multi-destination arrangement is that, as an approach to tourism development, it adds value to the tourism experience, while expanding the benefits of tourism to more than one destination. In this regard, multi-destination tourism can be considered one of the complementary means to diversify regional tourism industries while capitalizing on a region's natural and cultural assets and contributing to social and economic growth. From a regional perspective, given the increasing popularity of niche market tourism, a multi-destination travel option presents an opportunity for regional destinations to tap into new markets by promoting the natural, historic, and cultural attributes of each country. From a visitor's perspective, a multi-destination tourism package will afford travellers the opportunity to experience different destinations/localities, with each experience fulfilling a different desire of the visitor. In establishing multi-destination arrangements, critical mass will also be created for large investments in hotels and accommodations, attractions and sites development manufacturing, food production, and cultural and creative enterprises. Overall, more locals will become engaged in the tourism value chain, small- and medium-sized businesses will enter the market providing more goods, and services, more persons will be employed and more revenues will be generated for governments.

In spite of its tremendous potential to enhance tourism competitiveness within regions, there is a general recognition that successful multidestination arrangements require attention to certain factors. Establishing multi-destination arrangements will require that willingness and commitment on the part of the countries to coordinate marketing, product development, and investment strategies as one region while continuing to develop their unique attractions. Governments must work closely to examine the issues of tourism costs, air connectivity, the harmonization of visa policies, airspace usage, and pre-clearance arrangements. One possibility that can be effectively explored is adopting measures that would enable tourists to travel more conveniently to and among the countries within a region, such as visa waivers for select countries or a multiple-entry visa. Overall, regional governments and the private sector will need to collaborate more closely to advance market integration by fostering and harmonizing legislation on air connectivity, visa facilitation, product development, promotion, and human capital. Governments are also urged to explore incentives and strategies to strengthen regional carriers, enhance intra-regional travel, and through joint airlift agreements, increase linkages between regional and international airlines as part of a broad-based strategy to boost tourist arrivals.

References

Allan, David G. 2008. 'Jamaica's Golden Age.' *New York Times*. https://www.nytimes.com/2008/11/09/travel/09JamaicaWebSidebar.html.

Butler, R. 1980. 'When Jamaica Welcomed the World: The Great Exhibition of 1891.' *Jamaica Journal* 18 (3): 39–51.

Henry, B. 1987. 'Government Policy Initiatives in the Tourist Industry in Jamaica 1962-1987.' *The Weekend Star*, 26–27.

Johnson, Lauren C. 2014. 'Work at the Periphery: Issues of Tourism Sustainability in Jamaica.' *Culture Unbound Journal of Cultural Research*. 6 (20141001): 949.

Kingsbury, P. 2005. 'Jamaican Tourism and the Politics of Enjoyment.' *Geoforum* 36 (1): 113–32.

Koprčina, Lucia. 2020. '*Current State and Development Potential of Luxury Heritage Hospitality in Old City Center of Split, Croatia*.' Rochester Institute of Technology.

Martin, L. 1994. *Reflections on Jamaica's Tourism*. Montego Bay : Unlimited Exposures Limited.

Morris, Ainsworth. 2019. '12,000 New Hotel Rooms Over Five Years.' *Jamaica Information Service*. https://jis.gov.jm/12000-new-hotel-rooms-over-five-years/.

Salmon, Shanna K. 2022. 'Transformation of Jamaica's Tourism Sector.' *Jamaica Information Service*. https://jis.gov.jm/features/transformation-of-jamaicas-tourism-sector/.

Stankova, M., and S. Kaleichev. 2013. 'The Cutting Edge Between Mass and Luxury Tourism.' *Romanian Economic and Business Review* 1: 50–59.

Stupart, Copeland A., and Robert Shipley. 2013. 'Jamaica's Tourism: Sun, Sea and Sand to Cultural Heritage.' *Journal of Tourism Insights* 3 (1). https://doi.org/10.9707/2328-0824.1028.

Taylor, Frank Fonda. 2003. *To Hell with Paradise: A History of the Jamaican Tourist Industry*. Pittsburgh : University of Pittsburgh Press.

The Gleaner. 1995. *Geography and History of Jamaica*. Kingston: The Gleaner Company.

Index

U

V

Printed in the USA
CPSIA information can be obtained
at www.ICGtesting.com
JSHW080014230923
48890JS00003B/13

9 789768 2869